Lakȟótiya Wógla___ ___
Speak Lakota!

Level 1 Lakota Language Textbook

Háu tȟakóža.
Hiyú na Lakȟótiya wóglaka yo!

Tȟuŋkášila, Lakȟótiyapi uŋspémakhiya ye.

Lakota Language Consortium

Note: This is a dual teacher/student Lakota language textbook. It is designed to be used in conjunction with the Level 1 audio CD and the Level 1 Flashcard set.

Lakota Language Consortium, Inc., Pierre, SD and Bloomington, IN 47404
© 2004, 2012 by Lakota Language Consortium Inc.
All rights reserved.
First Printing 2004
Second Printing 2006
Third Printing 2008
Fourth Printing 2012
Fifth Printing 2016

ISBN: 0-9761082-0-8
ISBN-13: 978-0-9761082-0-7

Author: Jan Ullrich
Illustrations: František Valer
Layout: Jan Ullrich

The Lakota Language Consortium is a 501(c)3 tax-exempt nonprofit organization. Contributions are greatly appreciated and tax-deductible to the fullest extent of the law. Contact us at **contribute@lakhota.org** for more information.

Visit us at: **www.lakhota.org**
Textbook-related questions or comments may be sent to our language department at: **textbook@lakhota.org** or **jfu@lakhota.org** .

All rights reserved. No part of this publication may be reproduced or transmitted in any form or by any means, electronic or mechanical, including photocopy, recording, or any information storage and retrieval system, without permission in writing from the publisher.

Printed in China

This textbook would not have been possible without the assistance and determination of many people along the way. We would like to acknowledge our gratitude and appreciation to these people and organizations for helping in a variety of different ways to make this book possible:

John Around Him, Kayo Bad Heart Bull, Tim Bad Heart Bull, Elmer Bear Eagle, Evelyn Black Moon, Mark Bordeaux, Robert Brave Heart, Victor Brave Thunder, Richard Broken Nose, Wade Broken Nose, Gerda Brunner, Tom Casey, John Cedar Face, Bryan Charging Cloud, Joan Chief Eagle, Konstantin Chmelnicky, Cornelius Conroy, Less Duchenaux, Steve Dubray, Iris Dupris, Steve Emery, Mary Fire Thunder, Ed Flute, Melvin Grey Owl, Carol Ann Heart, Arlee High Elk, Betty High Elk, Suela High Elk, Vivian High Elk, Bryant High Horse, Reva High Horse, Peter Hill, Bernadette Hollow Horn, Fern Hollow Horn, Johnson Holy Rock, Twila Hopkins, Matthew Iron Hawk, Lyle Jack, Calvin Jumping Bull, Felix Kidder, David Konvičný, Philomine Lakota, Darleene Last Horse, Clara Lays Bad, Darrell Lays Bad, Gary Lays Bad, James Lays Bad, Shaina Lays Bad, Miriam Lays Bad, Christine Lejtay, Leonard Little Finger, Phinet Little White Man, Harry Little Thunder, Kevin Locke, Arlette Loud Hawk, Russel Loud Hawk, Catherine Looking Elk, Arvol Looking Horse, Ivan Looking Horse, Heike Meya, Wilhelm Meya, Elisabeth Makes Him First, Helmina Makes Him First, Wilmer Mesteth, Amanda Morrisette, the Oglala Sioux Tribe, the Oglala Nation Education Coalition, Gerald One Feather, Ingrid One Feather, Leola One Feather, Mary Ann Red Cloud, Emanuel Red Bear, Pat Red Elk, Gary Richards, David Rood, Paul Rooks, Alvin Slow Bear, Steve Slow Bear, Emerson Spider, Verola Spider, Darrel Standing Elk, Fred Stands, Edward Starr, Ivan Starr, John Steele, Petr Škaroupka, Delores Taken Alive, Jesse Taken Alive, Virgil Taken Alive, Babette Thin Elk, Chubbs Thunder Hawk, Sylvia Tobacco, Feleta Two Bulls, Sam Two Bulls, Robert Two Crow, Rick Two Dogs, Wilson Two Lance, Lenka Ullrichová, Matthew Uses the Knife, František Valer, Nina Webster, Loretta Whirlwind Horse, Roberta White, Alex White Plume, Clarence Wolf Guts, the school board of Wounded Knee District School, Vina Yankton, John Yellow Hawk, James Yellow Horse, Dennis Yellow Thunder, and all the other people that have helped and supported this project along the way. *Wóphila tȟáŋka.*

The author would like to express special thanks to Leonard Little Finger, Richard Broken Nose, Johnson Holy Rock and Wilhelm Meya for initiating and persevering with this language revitalization project. Many thanks also to David Rood, from the University of Colorado, Boulder, for invaluable comments on the linguistic aspects of the textbook.

An exhaustive page-by-page review of this textbook was undertaken by numerous Lakota individuals known to be language authorities. They all gave encouraging comments and positive assessments of the overall textbook structure. Whenever the reviewers provided local variations of words or phrases, we used the prevailing form and included the variations in the teacher's guide section. The following people approved of the language usage and cultural content:

John Around Him, Kayo Bad Heart Bull, Tim Bad Heart Bull, Richard Broken Nose, Calvin Jumping Bull, Christine Lajtay, Darrel Lays Bad, Gary Lays Bad, Leonard Little Finger, Catherine Looking Elk, Elisabeth Makes Him First, Wilmer Mesteth, Mary Ann Red Cloud, Verola Spider, Edward Starr, Wilson Two Lance, Matthew Uses the Knife, John Yellow Hawk, Russel Yellow Thunder.

Table of Contents

	Wóphila na Očháštȟaŋiŋpi Acknowledgements		1
	Introduction	An overview of the textbook methods and structure.	5
1.	Napéuŋkičhiyuzapi kte! Let's shake hands!	Greetings; introductions; self-identifications; gender endings; and Lakota oral vowels.	10
2.	Lé táku hwo/he? What is this?	Classroom objects; expressions in the negative; identifying objects; saying "yes" and "no" (**háŋ** and **hiyá**); and plain stops.	12
3.	Tóna hwo/he? How many?	Counting to twelve; describing age; simple time telling; days of the week; more classroom objects; and Lakota nasal vowels.	16
4.	Oówa tókča hwo/he? What color is it?	Colors in Lakota; describing the color of things; the verb forms: **bluhá**, **luhá**, **yuhá**; review of **Háŋ**, **Hiyá**; and aspirated **k**.	20
5.	Lé tókheča hwo/he? What does it look like?	Shapes, sizes; **lená**, **kiŋ**; plural inanimate color forms; review: colors, numbers; **bluhá**, **luhá**, **yuhá**; and sounds: **kȟ, kh**.	24
6.	Wóškate Toys	Basic terms for toys; reinforcement of **bluhá, luhá, yuhá**; colors and numbers; and sounds **pȟ, ph**.	28
7.	Hayápi Clothes	Basic clothing terms; verb **úŋ** – "to wear"; review of plural forms of colors; and sounds: **tȟ, th**.	32
8.	Thiwáhe Mitȟáwa kiŋ My Family	Basic kinship terms from male/female perspectives; verb form: **mayúkȟaŋ/mayúkȟe** – "I have"; describing kinship relationships; and sounds: **č, čh**.	36
9.	Mitȟáŋčhaŋ My Body	Basic body parts; reinforcing verb form **mayúkȟaŋ** – "I have"; and sounds: **s, š, z, ž**.	40
10.	Waskúyeča na Watȟótȟo Fruits and Vegetables	Common fruits and vegetables; the verb form: "I like"; and sounds: **bl, gm, gn, gl, mn** (voiced clusters).	42
11.	Lakȟóta Makȟóčhe kiŋ Lakota Country	Natural and geographic features of the countryside; the verb: "to see"; and sounds: **h, w, y, l, m, n**.	46
12.	Wóyute na Wóyatke Food and Drinks	Everyday foods and beverages; the verb forms: "I like" and "I am hungry"; and sounds: glottal stop.	50
13.	Obláye Ektá On the Plains	Animals of the plains; review of verb "to see"; and sounds: **č', k', p', t'** (ejective stops).	54

14.	Takúku Íčhitȟokeča Opposites	Antonyms; common descriptive terms; and sounds: consonant clusters.	58
15.	Wóžuthi Ektá On the Farm	Common animals around the farm; creating animate plural ending (**-pi**) for numbers, colors and the verb **héčha**; and sounds: more consonant clusters.	60
16.	Miíte My Face	Facial features; describing facial features; the verb: **yukȟáŋ** – "to have"; and sounds: more consonant clusters.	64
17.	Táku tókȟanuŋ hwo/he? What are you doing?	Basic verbs; the sentence structure **lowáŋ uŋmáspe** – "I know how to sing;" and sounds: more consonant clusters.	66
18.	Nitáku hwo/he? Who is this?	Terms for common persons and occupations; review of verbs and other vocabulary; review of "to see"; and sounds: more consonant clusters.	68
19.	Thiyáta At Home	Objects in a Lakota living room scene; review of kinship terms; and sounds: more consonant clusters.	70
20.	Wačhípi Ektá At a Pow-wow	Vocabulary associated with a pow-wow and pow-wow activities; review of kinship terms, traditional clothes, colors and sizes; and sounds: more consonant clusters.	74
21.	Otȟúŋwahe Ektá In Town	Terms associated with a town scene; review of "What do you see?" and "I see …"; and sounds: more consonant clusters.	78
22.	Tȟatúye Tópa Four Directions	Times of the year; seasons; weather; cardinal directions; and sounds: more consonant clusters.	82
23.	Ȟeyáta In the Mountains	Terms for alpine and forest animals; and sounds: more consonant clusters.	86
24.	Blé Ektá At the Lake	Terms for animals living in or near water; and sounds: more consonant clusters.	88
	Classrom Activities	Methods and ideas for introducing, practicing, and reinforcing vocabulary and sentence structure.	90
	Orthography and Pronunciation Guide	A technical and instructional guide to Lakota pronunciation and spelling.	94
	Glossary	English-Lakota glossary of terms used in each unit.	103
	Classroom Instructions in Lakota	Examples of common classroom phrases that help promote use of Lakota in class.	109
	Lakota Alphabet	A list of the 36-letter Lakota alphabet with Lakota example and English translation.	110

Dear Lakota educator and parent,

Our Lakota ways have been passed down to us for thousands of generations. Language is one of the most important of these. It embodies our prayers, our songs, our stories, and our ways. We need it to be truly Lakota. It lets us speak from the heart in the old ways.

Today, however, our language is in grave danger and very little time remains to rescue it. Your grandchildren and great-grandchildren need your help for it to survive. Your work is essential to raising a new generation of Lakota speakers before this happens.

There are many things that can be done to help stop the loss of our language. Some of the most important are using the language in the home and creating language proficiency and literacy in the schools. You can have an important role in making this happen. Through hard work and commitment to the language, it is possible to promote a new age group of Lakota speakers who will eventually raise their own children speaking Lakota. This must be the ultimate goal of all our work.

This textbook series is designed to help you teach children to become Lakota speakers using proven language-learning methods which imitate the natural language learning.

These tools will assist you in language instruction in the home and in the classroom. Preserving Lakota depends on individual people making the decision to use or to teach Lakota to the best of their abilities. As a teacher and parent, you have a distinctive role in saving our language and making it special for our *thakóža*. We hope you and your children enjoy these textbooks and that they become memorable experiences on the road to fluency.

Čhaŋtéwašteya napéčhiyuzape ló.

Yours Sincerely,

The Board of Directors

Lakota Language Consortium

This is the first volume in a series of Lakota language textbooks. It is designed for the youngest learners – kindergarten to grade three. With minor alteration, it can also be used successfully in higher grades, especially in cases where the students have had little, or no, structured Lakota instruction. Similarly, it can be utilized by adult self-learners at the beginner level.

It should be noted that this textbook is not a grammar. It does not attempt to list or explain paradigms of verb inflection or other grammatical rules. Its main goal is to provide contextualized and sequenced teaching material in a way that introduces basic beginning Lakota semantic categories and associated sentence structures.

The other purpose of this book is to provide a tool to help teachers introduce vocabulary and sentence patterns through age-appropriate and effective methods.

The lesson units in this textbook are sequenced in a way that builds upon material from earlier units. Lessons should, therefore, be utilized in the given order. We recommend that this textbook be used with a Lakota language class that meets four to five times weekly, with three times being the absolute minimum.

Format of the Textbook

This book is a combination of a textbook, picture dictionary, activity book, and teacher's guide. All units begin with an introductory page (referred to as the Lesson Page) that provides context for the new vocabulary (usually in the form of a full page illustration). The following page provides detailed instructions for teachers and parents, and suggestions for additional activities. Additional activities, like coloring, provide children with needed breaks and help them relate to the new vocabulary and sentence structure.

Teacher's Guide

An integral part of the textbook is the teacher's guide. It consists of this brief introduction to the teaching methods, instructions for each of the lessons, a guide for teaching activities (page 90), and an orthography and pronunciation guide (page 96). It is very important that teachers familiarize themselves with all these sections before they start using the textbook. Instructions for the individual lesson units are located directly within those units. This structure provides teachers with easy access to the lesson guidelines during classes and supports the use of the teacher's guide. Parents should also take advantage of this section as a way to go through some of the lessons with their children at home.

In the teacher's guide, braces {} provide an English translation to the preceding Lakota phrase or word. This translation is not intended to be spoken or written during the classroom activities.

An important part of this Lakota language program is the initial teacher training workshop offered for the involved teachers before the beginning of each school year. During these workshops, teachers are introduced to the teaching methods in a more detailed way than is possible in this brief introduction.

Teaching Methods

Teachers need to be aware that teaching a language to young children has very specific demands. Students on the K-1 level are not familiar with classification for parts of speech and other language related terminology. Because abstract thinking skills are not highly developed at this age, children relate to and acquire new vocabulary best when they are able to see and touch the items whose names they hear. The more senses that are employed, the more learning will occur. The theoretical basis of this textbook is that vocabulary is introduced through pictures and reinforced contextually.

The methodology of this textbook is based on the phases of natural language acquisition. At first the children only listen; then they respond physically to words they recognize (TPR – Total Physical Response); later they use single words in place of whole sentences. At this stage children are more likely to react to a question rather than to talk on their own.

Therefore, young students learn a language in four stages:

1. Seeing, touching and **hearing**
2. Recognizing (Point at!, Show me!, Find!, Touch!)
3. Understanding ("yes" and "no" questions - *Is this white?*; "or" questions –*Is this large or small?*, commands - *Take this!, Go there!*; and other simple sentences etc.)
4. **What is this? Describing that**. (More complex sentences used actively by the students.)

In a classroom environment, young students can attain stage three (i.e. passive understanding). Stage four should not be the ultimate goal of teaching children of K-1 age. The passive knowledge gained by stage one to three is a very good base for later advancement towards active speaking. This approach mirrors the natural progress of language acquisition, in which the silent period takes up to three years.

The methods employed in this course are largely based on using flashcards. Both the teacher and the children will perform many different kinds of activities with them. Sometimes they will hold them in their hands but frequently the teachers will need to exhibit them in a place easily seen by all the children. A magnetic board is ideal for this. Alternatively they could use a large corkboard and pin the flashcards, or they may stretch a line along a wall and clothespin the cards to it. It is also very useful to have more than one place in the classroom where they can exhibit the flashcards.

Because abstract comprehension is not part of a typical early elementary student's cognitive toolbox, grammar rules and sentence patterns should be demonstrated rather than explained. Children learn by doing things rather than thinking about them. They can master various sentence patterns and grammatical rules best by hearing and practicing them frequently. Nevertheless, the subconscious knowledge of some simple grammar rules can still be strengthened by simple motivating questions. For instance, after a lesson demonstrating the question-making enclitic "**he**", the teacher can ask: "Children, what do you think this 'he' stands for?" – Children are likely to respond: "It makes a question," or, "It is for asking questions."

For children, language acquisition is more an emotional and social enterprise, rather than an intellectual one. Therefore, learning activities should, whenever possible, imitate real life situations and family environments.

Teachers should make sure that classmates do not ridicule another student's pronunciation performance. This can be extremely discouraging for young learners (and learners in general) and can lead to an unconscious dislike or fear of the subject. Feeling safe is one of the most important things a child can feel while learning a new language. Therefore, in the classroom and in any teaching or learning activity teachers should develop a secure environment where students can feel both cared for and excited about speaking the language.

It is very important that teachers continue giving the children positive feedback in spite of the quality of their performance or progress. Criticism can be very discouraging for young students in this sensitive phase.

There are many ways that teachers can correct a student's errors in gentle and reassuring ways. For example, after a child makes a mistake, the teacher can repeat the word or sentence correctly (with a smile on his/her face) and with a praising word, such as "wašté" (good) for other things that were done well. Additionally, the teachers can say something like this: "Wašté (good), now try to say it after me again with better pronunciation."

The reading and writing portions of this textbook were designed for upper elementary students as way to allow the textbook to be flexibly used at those levels before the sequels are produced. At the early elementary level, children should not be required to acquire writing ability in Lakota. Therefore, this textbook encourages students to read and to recognize words (e.g. by matching them with pictures). Students will also be asked to copy words rather than write independently.

The joy of teaching young children is that they learn much faster than adults do. Unfortunately, children also forget things much faster then adults. This is why it is necessary to constantly repeat, review and reinforce the learned vocabulary and sentence patterns (the three R's of language learning). These are best accomplished through a variety of activities, which keep children motivated.

Young children often have trouble concentrating on one type of activity for a long time. If any activity becomes too long or repetitive, they lose interest in it and no longer pay attention. In that case, they either start becoming apathetic or find something else to do. Some teachers may believe that such behavior indicates lack of intelligence or self-control. However, it is natural for children to react in this way.

Considering all this, the language teacher is advised to be empathetic with the children and on constant alert for such tendencies. If a significant number of students become restless or lose their interest in what is going on, a change in activity should take place. Very often, students can be re-stimulated by an activity involving the Total Physical Response approach, such as "point at", "stand up" etc.

The teacher's guide occasionally suggests a specific series of activities in each unit. Teachers should monitor themselves and allow for breaks or changes to a different type of activity. The activities suggested in the teacher's guide section should be evenly distributed in lessons throughout the week. This technique encourages constant reviewing.

Small children often lack adult-type self-control. They cannot remain completely still for any significant length of time and get easily over-excited when they have a chance to be active. It helps to use methods that both involve children actively and those that provide quiet time. Active techniques like moving around the classroom, singing, interactions, and TPR, provide a dynamic atmosphere, stimulating the children. Calm-inducing techniques, such as coloring, drawing, writing, and copying, provide children with time to process concepts learned earlier and to rest between active periods. Teachers who carefully balance these two types of activities achieve a healthy kind of learning that brings out the best in children.

Introducing, exercising, or reinforcing vocabulary and sentences through English should be avoided as much as possible. Translating from one language to another is a complex process that is difficult even for adults. Translation has rarely been an effective means for teaching a language.

Finally, please remember that the most important thing that teachers can do is to be patient and empathetic when working with young children.

Classroom Instructions in Lakota

Teachers should use as much Lakota as possible when interacting with the child. They can find a list of useful classroom instructions and expressions in Lakota on page 109.

Consistent use of classroom instructions in Lakota is one of the many methods that contextualize vocabulary and sentence structure.

Content of the Book

The lesson units in this book are built around themes and topics that reflect the culture and local natural environment. The thematic topics in this book try to cover the most immediate surroundings of the child.

Each unit presents a set of words of the particular theme or semantic domain. Children naturally learn nouns easiest and the structure of this textbook reflects this. Nevertheless, each unit also introduces one or two verbs and a sentence structure, so that the nouns can be used in sentences and in dialogues that contextualize the vocabulary.

Teaching the Culture

It is very important to include cultural content in language teaching, while also being age-appropriate. Some of the more intellectual or spiritual parts of Lakota culture should become part of language teaching only when students are ready for it. We should remember that children want to be able to talk in Lakota about things in their own world – about toys, games, sports, and other things that they do. These two aspects of language teaching have to be balanced so that children will be motivated to learn the language. This textbook is aimed at teaching culture by teaching language proficiency.

Culture is encoded in language and people learning languages are automatically acquiring knowledge of culture as they learn to speak. Still, it is sometimes useful to provide cultural learning during language lessons. This can be best done by incorporating cultural learning into activities in the Lakota language.

Subdialects and Local Variants

Lakota is spoken slightly differently in different communities (these varieties are usually called "sub-dialects"). Identified local variants are addressed in the "For Teachers and Parents" section. Teachers and parents are encouraged to employ the variants used in their community or area whenever they arise. In this case, teachers should explain to their students that a different word is used in their community than the one presented.

We believe it is important to have respect for variations, thus honoring the richness of Lakota language and culture in its entirety.

Next Volumes

Finally, this is the first volume in a series of textbooks. Students will be able to advance levels on a year-by-year basis. Teachers, however, are still encouraged to continue to use this volume for higher grades to help reinforce topics and semantic domains.

The beginning stage is the most important part in learning a language

Early elementary learners need enthusiastic and lively teachers who are willing to do playful activities with them. They learn largely by playing and they appreciate teachers who are able to join them while still maintaining the position of teacher and organizer.

The beginning stage of learning a language is very important. If Lakota classes become boring for the children, they are likely to keep that impression with them for a long time. However, if a teacher can make the class interesting, fun and playful, then children will be motivated to continue learning the language. This approach should, with any luck, enable them to enjoy studying the deeper meanings of their language and culture as they grow older.

Additional Activities and Support for Teachers

The Lakota Language Consortium web-site (www.lakhota.org) provides additional resources and ideas for teaching activities, methods and classroom advice. New activities will be continually updated.

Useful tools can also be found there, such as special fonts with characters for Lakota, a Lakota language spellchecker for MicrosoftWord®, printable sheets with tests and additional exercises, and printable flashcards.

Orthography (Spelling)

This textbook uses an orthography that consistently marks each of the meaningful sounds of the language with a distinct symbol. Because of this, it is easy to learn and use. It has been tested with students of various ages and has proven to be very effective. Students are able to read this orthography consistently without

problems and find it simple to learn. Some of the primary reasons include:

- Nasal vowels and aspirated stops are represented by letters rather than diacritics; therefore:
- The orthography is easy to write and type.
- It represents differences between similar words more clearly, such as **maká** "skunk" vs. **makȟá** "earth"; and **kíza** "squeak" vs. **khíza** "to fight", etc.
- It uses internationally-recognized characters which are available as Unicode fonts.
- It is consistent – each sound is assigned to a character (this makes it easier for children and students to read and write every word properly). Consistent phonetic orthography makes pronunciation of written words perfectly predictable.

The main characteristics of the orthography are:
- Instead of multiple diacritics only one is employed:

   ǧ, ȟ, š, ž as opposed to g, h, s, z

- Stress is marked consistently: **eyáya** "he kept saying" vs. **éyaya** "he took it away" etc.
- Aspirated stops are differentiated from plain stops by letters **h** and **ȟ** rather than by diacritics, e.g.:

tó "yes" vs. **tȟó** "blue"
kéya "he said that" vs. **khéya** "snapping turtle"

The orthography is explained in detail on page 96. In that section teachers can find instructions and suggestions on how to teach reading, writing, and pronunciation in Lakota.

1. Napéuŋkičhiyuzapi kte! Let's shake hands!

Háu! Háu!

| hokšíla | hokšíla |

Háŋ! Háŋ!

| wičhíŋčala | wičhíŋčala |

Háu! Háŋ!

| hokšíla | wičhíŋčala |

1. Táku eníčiyapi hwo?

2. Lisa emáčiyapi.

4. Robert emáčiyape ló.

3. Na níš táku eníčiyapi he?

Toníktuka he?
Lisa High Eagle hé miyé.
Lakȟóta wičhíŋčala hemáčha kštó.
Pine Ridge hemátaŋhaŋ.

Matáŋyaŋ yeló!
Robert Jumping Bear hé miyé.
Lakȟóta hokšíla hemáčha yeló.
Nitúwe hwo?

Can you guess what these children are saying? If not, ask your teacher.
Can you say these things about yourself?

Vocabulary on pg. 103.
Sounds: Lakota oral vowels, pg. 96.

The opening page of this unit introduces greetings used by boys (and men) "**háu**" and by girls (and women) "**háŋ**." In the traditional Lakota social environment, greetings were usually accompanied by kinship terms (these will be introduced later). Traditionally, women used "**háŋ**" only in response to a greeting. More recently, this word has become a part of regular greeting as children of both sexes are taught to say greetings.

- **Háu / Háŋ**

To begin, ask the children to shake hands (**napékičhiyuza po!**) in pairs and greet each other with **háu** or **háŋ**.

- **Táku eníčiyapi hwo/he?**

Write this sentence on the board and then demonstrate like this: Point at yourself (or put the palm of your hand on your chest) and say:
[Your name] emáčiyapi.
Then point with your hand to one of the children and say:
Táku eníčiyapi hwo/he?
Help the child answer, e.g.: **[David] emáčiyapi.**
Practice with all children in the classroom. Then ask them this: "Children, do you know how to say, 'What is your name?' in Lakota?"
They should be able to say: **Táku eníčiyapi hwo/he?**
Then ask them to question and answer each other about their names in Lakota.
After the children are familiar with these sentences you may add the use of gender endings, **emáčiyape ló** for boys and **emáčiyapi kštó** for girls.

- Point at the characters of Robert and Lisa on the left hand page and say this:
Lé hokšíla héčha.
Lé wičhíŋčala héčha.

- Then point at a boy and a girl in the classroom and repeat the two sentences.
Point at the character of Robert and Lisa again and play the audio CD with their dialogue. Then say:
Hokšíla kiŋ Robert ečíyapi.
Wičhíŋčala kiŋ Lisa ečíyapi.
Ask the children to repeat each of the sentences.

- Point at one of the children in the classroom and ask:
Hokšíla kiŋ lé táku ečíyapi hwo/he?
The children answer:
Gerry ečíyapi. or **Hokšíla kiŋ (lé) Gerry ečíyapi.**
Repeat the activity pointing at other children.

- Then call on a child and ask him/her something like this, while pointing at another student:
Teacher: Peter! Hokšíla kiŋ lé táku ečíyapi hwo/he?
Peter: Hokšíla kiŋ Ron ečíyapi.

Then ask the children to point at one of their classmates and ask you about his or her name:

Hokšíla / Wičhíŋčala kiŋ lé táku ečíyapi hwo/he?
or: **Hé táku ečíyapi hwo/he?**

With third graders and older students you can also teach and practice these sentences (only in Lakota):
Nitúwe hwo/he? {Who are you?} ➔ **Robert Crow hé miyé.** {I am Robert Crow.}
Nitáku hwo/he? {What are you?} ➔ **Hokšíla/Wičhíŋčala hemáčha.** {I am a boy/girl.} or **Homákšila.** {I am a boy.} / **Wimáčhiŋčala** {I am a girl.}
Toníktuka hwo/he? {How are <u>you</u>?} / **Toníkheča hwo/he?** {How are <u>you</u>?} ➔ **Matáŋyaŋ yeló/kštó.** {<u>I am</u> fine.}
Taŋyáŋ glá yo/ye (po/pe)! {Good bye!, "Go home well!"}
Tókša akhé. {Later again.}

In order not to confuse the children, these questions and their corresponding answers should be taught and practiced one at a time.

The English translations provided in braces {} are for reference only and are not intended to be spoken out loud in the classroom. Arrows (➔) indicate a response in a dialogue sequence.

Gender endings will also be introduced, but only in a passive way – so that children understand them. They should start using them actively only after they are familiar with the sentence structure. Most reviewers agreed that **yeló** and **kštó/ye** add strong assertion and that children don't use them as often as adults do.

After this unit, the children should be able to say the following sentences in Lakota: "What is your/his/her name?," "How are you?," and "Good bye." They should also be able to say: **(Lakȟóta) hokšíla / wičhíŋčala hemáčha.** {I am a (Lakota) boy/girl.}

Note 1: Some contemporary materials by native speakers (e.g. Albert White Hat) state that the question word "**he**" is only used by women, while men always use "**hwo**" or "**huŋwó.**" Though this may be true in some communities, it is not the case among most current speakers in Pine Ridge. Also, all historic materials (such as texts collected by Deloria, Buechel and others), as well as contemporary studies document that "**he**" is used by both sexes. The enclitic **hwo/huŋwó** is used by men only in formal situations. Teachers should teach whatever usage is common in their communities.
Note 2: The word **wičhíŋčala** {girl} is sometimes spelled **wiŋčhíŋčala.**
Note 3: Teachers may want to introduce the students to the fast speech pronunciation of **Táku eníčiyapi he?,** which is **Tág eníčiyab he?**
Note 4: The definite article may be pronounced either as **kiŋ** or **ki.** This textbook attempts to follow the more traditional spelling **kiŋ.**

11

Vocabulary of this unit is on page n. 103.

Lé wówapi héčha. (write this on the board)

• Pick up various objects and say Lakota sentences like: Lé (wówapi) héčha.

• Write the words lé, wówapi and héčha in a column on the blackboard. Then ask the children if they know what the words mean. Praise them if they do, help them if they don't: lé {this}, wówapi {book}, héčha {it is (such)}.

• Then use flashcard activities and games (page 90–93) to teach the new words.

• Ask the children to find the things learned on the first page of this lesson, point at them and say their Lakota name. Ask them to notice how the words are written. (Alternatively, play the audio CD and ask the children to point at the things they hear named).

• Have the children do the coloring activity on the following page (the children should be able to recognize the words and color the items accordingly).

Lé táku hwo/he? (write this on the board)

• While holding up the previously taught classroom objects ask: Lé táku hwo/he?

• (The children should be able to guess the meaning of the sentence, if they can't, demonstrate the answer. This should help them understand the context. Do not translate the sentence into English.)

• Ask Lé táku hwo/he? about several objects.

• Write the words lé, táku and hwo/he? in a column on the blackboard. Then ask the children if they know what the words mean. Praise them if they do, help them if they don't: lé {this}, táku {what}, hwo/he? {question}.

• Then ask the children to point at objects (or hold them) and ask you with Lé táku hwo/he?

• Tell the children that now they know the Lakota question Lé táku hwo/he? and therefore they can ask their parents or grandparents in Lakota about various things. This should be done at the end of class.

Start the next class by reviewing the previous one (vocabulary, Lé …. héčha., Lé táku hwo/he?).

Sounds – Plain Stops

Plain stops (č, k, p, t) are among the most common Lakota consonants, but are very rare in English. Early correct and consistent practicing of their pronunciation is essential for learning the Lakota language. The textbook introduces plain stops before aspirated stops. This keeps students from tending to pronounce stops the way they sound in English. Follow the instructions on page 96 to teach plain stops.

"Yes" and "No" (Háŋ and Hiyá)

Take out 6 flashcards of previously learned vocabulary and show them to the children (they say the words).

• Choose one of the flashcards but make sure children don't see which one you have.

• Tell them to guess the card you chose by saying the Lakota word (make sure you only call on one child at a time).

• If the word isn't correct, shake your head "no" very clearly and say: Hiyá.

• If a child guesses the word correctly, nod your head "yes" very clearly and say: Háŋ. At the same time show the card.

• Play this game 3 or 4 times, with different sets of flashcards

After several rounds ask the children this question:

• Children, what do you think the Lakota word is for "Yes"?

• Children should be able to say Háŋ.

• Children, what do you think the Lakota word is for "No"?

• Children should be able to say Hiyá.

• Put the labels (or write the words) of Háŋ and Hiyá on the board and pronounce them clearly again. Children repeat.

Ask the children to do the activities on the second activity page. With older or more advanced students you can also teach the sentence Lé wówapi (héčha) šni. – This is not a book.

Note 1: lé versus hé: The distinction between "this" (lé, within arm's length) and "that" (hé, outside of arm's length) is not addressed in this textbook. Teachers should judge whether their students are ready for this concept. If so, they should demonstrate it by holding and/or pointing at objects and saying Lé táku hwo/he? and Hé táku hwo/he? The answers use lé or hé depending on the distance of the one who answers from the object.

Note 2: The sentence Lé wówapi héčha. {This is a book.} can also be said without héčha: Lé wówapi. The verb héčha is only used to describe an object; it is not used for identification.

Note 3: In yes/no questions in English there is a rising pitch at the end of the question. This is never the case in Lakota – melody of the sentence always falls on hwo/he. Make sure the children don't pronounce questions in Lakota with rising pitch.

Note 4: The original meaning of wakšíča is "bowl", while "plate" is wakšíča blaská. For the sake of simplicity we use wakšíča as the generic term for dish.

Note 5: Oákaŋke is a more recent form of oákaŋyaŋke.

Note 6: Variations of "chalkboard" are čhaŋbláska, čhaŋbláska akáŋwowapi, čhaŋbláska wówapi, él-wówapi.

Note 7: Some people differentiate between wíčazo {pencil} and mnísapa wíčazo {pen}, but most use wíčazo as a generic term.

Note 8: Two reviewers gave the word wíyukse for "scissors".

wówapi   wíčazo   iyúšla   oákaŋke   wíyatke

akáŋwowapi   itówapi   wóžuha   čhaŋbláska   wakšíča

2. Lé táku hwo/he? Connect the words with the pictures.

 wówapi
wíyatke wíčazo iyúšla oákaŋke

wóžuha čhaŋbláska itówapi wakšíča akáŋwowapi

3. Háŋ naíŋš hiyá? Yes or no?

Lé **wówapi** héčha hwo/he?   Háŋ (Hiyá)

Lé **wíyatke** héčha hwo/he?   Háŋ Hiyá

Lé **wíčazo** héčha hwo/he?   Háŋ Hiyá

Lé **iyúšla** héčha hwo/he?  Háŋ Hiyá

Lé **wakšíča** héčha hwo/he?   Háŋ Hiyá

Lé **wóžuha** héčha hwo/he?   Háŋ Hiyá

Lé **čhaŋbláska** héčha hwo/he?   Háŋ Hiyá

Lé **akáŋwowapi** héčha hwo/he?   Háŋ Hiyá

Lé **oákaŋke** héčha hwo/he?   Háŋ Hiyá

15

1	2	3	4	5	6	5	4	3	2	1

wíyatke **wanží**   wíyatke **núnpa**   wíyatke yámni

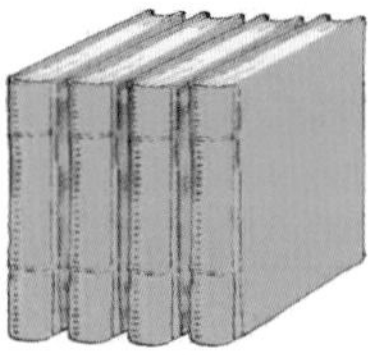

wówapi tópa    wówapi **záptan**   wówapi šákpe

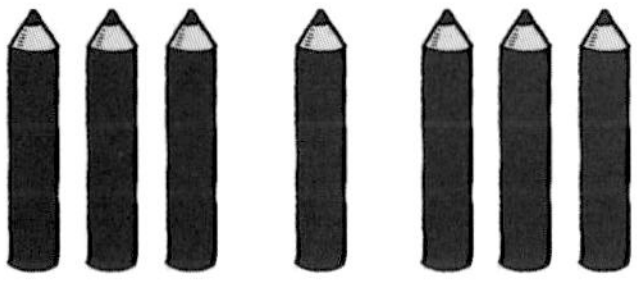

wíčazo **šakówin**   wíčazo **šaglóǧan**   wíčazo napčíyunka

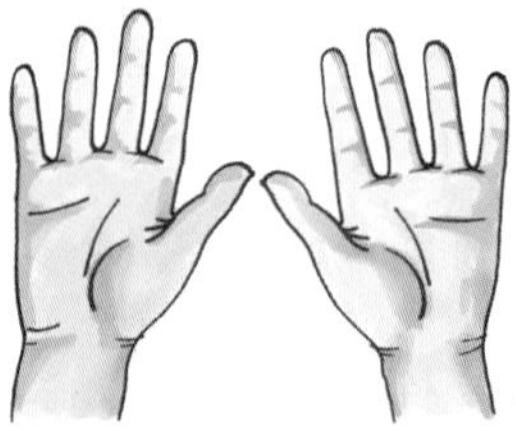

napsúkaza wikčémna   mázaškanškan **akéwanží**   mázaškanškan **akénunpa**

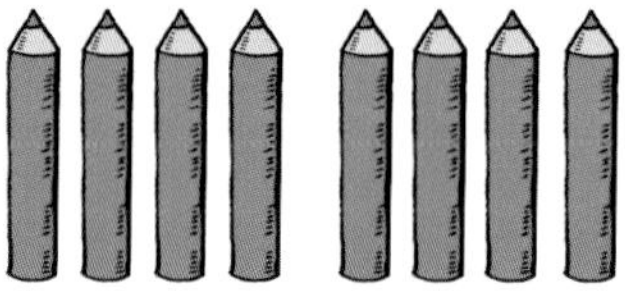

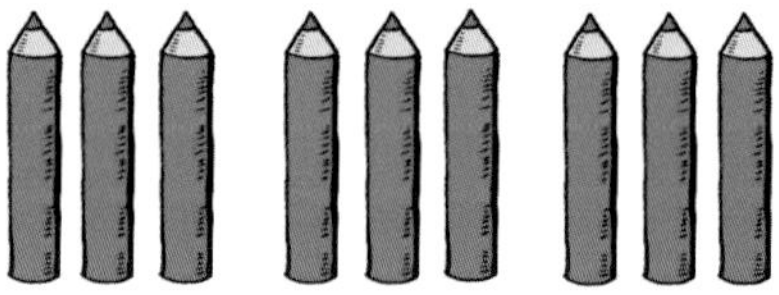

7	8	9	10	11	12	11	10	9	8	7

1. Waníyetu **ni**tóna hwo?

2. Waníyetu **ma**šákowin.

4. Waníyetu **ma**šákpe.

3. Na níš?
Waníyetu **ni**tóna he?

Waníyetu –
"winter" or "year".
What are the
children saying?

Can you ask your
classmate the same
question? And can you
answer?

16

Vocabulary on pg. 103.

Sounds: nasal vowels (instructions for teaching nasal vowels on pg. 97).

Practice pronunciation of nasal vowels: **aŋ, iŋ, uŋ**.

With 2nd – 3rd graders you can practice writing **aŋ, iŋ, uŋ**.

- **Teaching numbers 1 to 6**

Use cards with digits and practice the pronunciation of Lakota numbers 1 to 6. You may also use the audio CD. Order the numbers in forward and backward sequences of 1–2–3–4–5–6 and 6–5–4–3–2–1. Once the children are able to say these sequences well, practice the numbers at random.

- **Work with the Lesson Page (numbers 1–6)**

Hold the Lesson Page towards the children. Point at the first picture and say:

Wíyatke waŋží.

Children repeat after you while pointing at one picture at a time: **wíyatke waŋží; wíyatke núŋpa**, etc.

- **Break**

At this point let the children relax from active learning by doing the exercises on the following page (exercises dealing with numbers 1–6).

After the break or in the next class: **Tóna hwo/he?**

Hold the Lesson Page towards the children. Point at a picture and say: **Tóna hwo/he?**

Demonstrate the answer by saying the number of objects in the picture, e.g.: **Yámni.**

Point at another picture and ask again (**Tóna hwo/he?**). Children answer using only the number.

- **Teaching numbers 7 to 12**

Teach the numbers 7 to 12 the same way as 1–6 previously.

- **Tóna hwo/he?**

Use the same exercises for **Tóna hwo/he?** as previously, for 7 to 12 and for 1 to 12.

- **Break**

Let the children relax by doing exercises dealing with numbers 7 to 12 on the second activity page.

After the break or in the next class:

- **Play games with numbers**

1) Bingo

The children each have cards sets numbered 1 to 12 or card sets of images in multiples of 1 to 12 (you can create these cards by copying the Lesson Page and letting the children color the objects).

The children put the cards in rows and columns 3 by 4 in a random order.

You will then say numbers in Lakota and they will turn over the card with the appropriate number. The child that has a full row or column turned over first wins and

says "BINGO!" Play as long as the children are enjoying themselves.

2) Use ten to twelve flashcards of previously taught vocabulary (classroom items). Put the flashcards on the board and number them from 1 to 12.

Say the name of each of the items and ask the children to say its number. Then switch, say the numbers, and have the children say the items.

If the children are old enough to know the digits and their values, use cards with the Lakota words for 1 to 12 and ask the children to match these with digits (e.g. on the board, on their desks etc.)

- **Waníyetu nitóna hwo/he?**

Let the children look at the dialogue at the bottom of the Lesson Page. Play the audio CD with the dialogue twice. (You may also read it.) Then point at the boy in the picture and say:

Lé táku hwo/he? ➔ **Hokšíla.**

Hé waníyetu tóna hwo/he? ➔ **(Waníyetu) šákpe.**

Ask the children: "Do you know how to say 'I am six'?" Some children should answer with "**mašákpe.**"

Then ask: "Do you know how to say, 'I am six years old.'?" ➔ **Waníyetu mašákpe.** "How do we say 'How old are you?'?" ➔ **Waníyetu nitóna hwo/he?**

Then ask several children:

Hokšíla, waníyetu nitóna hwo/he?

Wičhíŋčala, waníyetu nitóna hwo/he?

Afterwards have the children practice the dialogue in pairs. Another way of telling age is using the verb **henákeča**: **Waníyetu wikčémna henámakeča.** {I am ten years old.}

- **Mázaškaŋškaŋ tóna hwo/he?**

With more advanced or older children you may be able to teach time telling. Use a paper clock with movable hands or pictures with 1 to 12 o'clock. Practice saying:

Mázaškaŋškaŋ tóna hwo/he? ➔ **Mázaškaŋškaŋ núŋpa.**

Ask the children as you point at a picture (clock). Then let them ask you while pointing at a clock.

You may also use the expression **Oápȟe/Owápȟe tóna hwo/he?** for "What time is it?"

(As a further way of reviewing numbers, teach days of the week (create labels for them).)

- **What can you say about yourself?**

See if some children can say three sentences about themselves such as:

Robert Gray Eagle emáčiyapi.

Hokšíla hemáčha yeló. Waníyetu mašákowiŋ.

Note: Some reviewers indicated that **waŋží** is used to express the number of objects (e.g. 'one book'), while **wáŋči** is used for counting. Others felt there was no such distinction.

1. Connect the numbers with the correct words!

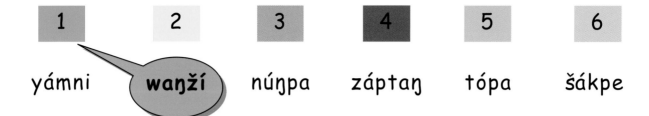

| 1 | 2 | 3 | 4 | 5 | 6 |

yámni   **waŋží**   núŋpa   záptaŋ   tópa   šákpe

2. Read, circle and connect!

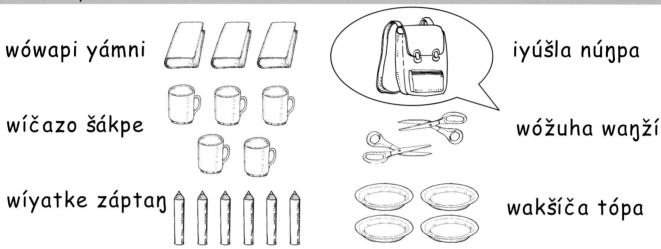

wówapi yámni

wíčazo šákpe

wíyatke záptaŋ

iyúšla núŋpa

wóžuha waŋží

wakšíča tópa

3. Lená tóna hwo/he? How many are there? (The numbers reveal the colors.)

waŋží   núŋpa   yámni   tópa   záptaŋ   šákpe

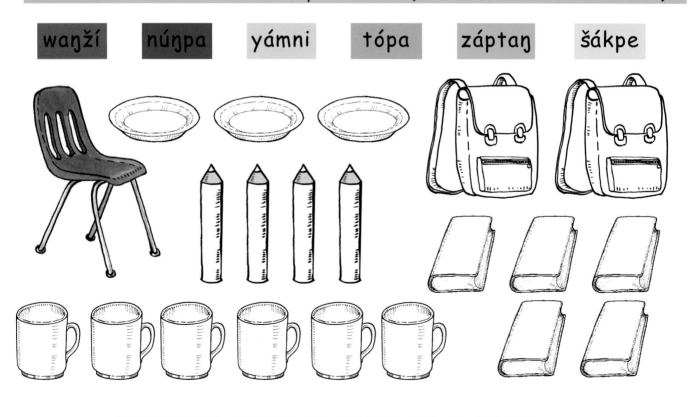

| wówapi | oákaŋke | wíyatke | wakšíča | wóžuha | wíčazo |

18

4. Connect the numbers with the words.

7	8	9	10	11	12

šaglóǧaŋ šakówiŋ napčíyuŋka akéwaŋží wikčémna akénuŋpa

5. Tóna hwo/he?   How many? (The numbers reveal the colors.)

šakówiŋ	šaglóǧaŋ	napčíyuŋka	wikčémna	akéwaŋží	akénuŋpa

6. Tóna hwo/he?   How many?

waŋží   núŋpa   yámni   tópa   záptaŋ   šákpe

šakówiŋ   šaglóǧaŋ   napčíyuŋka   wikčémna   akéwaŋží   akénuŋpa

Can you find these pictures?

| Šúŋka **sápe**   Kimímela **šá**   Zíškopela **zí**   Gnašká **tȟózi**   Igmú **ǧí** |

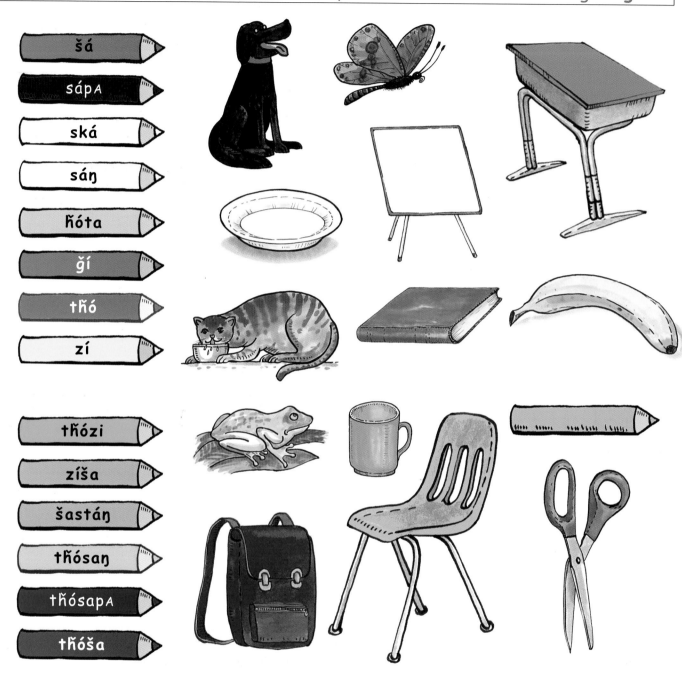

1. This is a white and black feather. What color are the other things?

Wíyaka kiŋ lé **ská** <u>na</u> **sápe**.

Vocabulary on pg. 103;
Sounds: ȟ and ǧ (see instructions on pg. 97).
Balance the dialogue activities with the exercise pages at the end of the unit.

1. Colors

• There are 14 words for colors in this lesson. To begin, teach the first 8 colors and then the remaining 6 (They are compounds of the first 8).

• Use flashcards activities (page 90–93) to teach the new vocabulary.

• Review the numbers: put 10 to 12 flashcards of colors on the board and number them. Ask the children to say the number of the color you name. Switch the activity, you say numbers, the children say the colors.

2. Colors on the Lesson Page

• Once the children know the colors very well, work with this unit's Lesson Page. The children should open their books and look at the page. Ask them to say the Lakota word of an animal or thing whose color you will say, e.g.: teacher: tȟó; children: wówapi. (Start with the first 8 colors, then add the remainder.)

• Do the same activity, this time you say the items and the children say the colors.

• **Demonstrate** the following question and answer dialogue (perhaps with an advanced student):
Q: **Wówapi kiŋ lé oówa tókča hwo/he?** {What color is the book?}
A: **(Wówapi kiŋ lé) tȟó.** {It is blue (The book is blue.)}

• In the K-1 level use the simpler question while pointing at the item (**Lé oówa tókča hwo/he?** {What color is this?}) and let the children give a short answer (**Lé šá.** {This is red.}) With older students elicit the full sentences by having the children ask each other the question (e.g. **Wíčazo kiŋ lé oówa tókča hwo/he?**).
Avoid describing plural objects. The plural forms of the colors will be introduced in later chapters (inanimate plural cf. Unit 5, animate plural cf. Unit 15).

• Have the children work in pairs or in groups of 3 to 4. They should ask each other: **Lé oówa tókča hwo/he?** about the different things in the textbook and in the classroom.

3. Modifier Position

In this unit the children are introduced for the first time to the position of a modifier (i.e. color). Because the position differs from that in English, it is important to demonstrate and practice it extensively. Do not explain it, but demonstrate it repeatedly.

• Ask the children to point at the picture you name. (**Oákaŋke makípazo wo!**).

• Then name the individual pictures on the first page of the unit, e.g.:
Lé wówapi <u>tȟó</u>.; Lé igmú <u>ǧí</u>.; Lé wakšíča <u>ská</u>. etc.

• Now change the activity. Point at a picture (or a classroom object) and ask **Lé táku hwo/he?** The children should describe it with a noun and modifier.

• If you think the children grasped the modifier position well enough, have them do similar activity in pairs or groups.

4. Na = And

Demonstrate the use of **na** {and} with objects of multiple color. Hold up a multicolored object and say slowly and carefully a phrase like: **Lé wóžuha kiŋ tȟó na šá.** {This bag is blue and red.}.
Repeat with other objects. Ask the children: "Children, do you know how we say 'and' in Lakota?"
Ask the children to point to other multicolored objects and describe them, e.g.: **Lé wówapi tȟózi na zí.**

5. Review "Yes" and "No" (Háŋ and Hiyá)

Ask about pictures or classroom objects. Have the children answer with **Háŋ** and **Hiyá** like this:
Šúŋka kiŋ lé ská hwo/he? {Is the dog white?} ➔ **Hiyá** {No.}
Wówapi kiŋ lé tȟó hwo/he? ➔ **Háŋ**.
Iyúšla kiŋ lé tȟóša hwo/he? ➔ **Háŋ**. etc.

The introduction of **kiŋ** should be passive. Children are not expected to use it themselves. With the upper grades, you can practice this actively – the students can ask similar questions in their work groups. They may use a structure like:
Šúŋka kiŋ lé ská hwo/he?

Note 1: The question, **Oówa tókča hwo/he?** is not a phrase recognized by all communities. Lakota speakers working with the Colorado Lakhota Project used this phrase for asking color of non-animate objects. David Little Elk uses the phrase for both inanimate objects and animals. The reviewers of this textbook were less absolute about its use, especially in the context of the color of birds. **Híŋtokča hwo/he?** was given for fur bearing animals.
Note 2: In some communities **ȟóta** has a changeable "A" (**ȟótA**). When used at the end of sentences and before some enclitics (such as **šni**) **ȟótA** becomes **ȟóte** in these communities and among some individuals.
Note 3: The word for "pink" is **šastáŋ** in some communities, and **šasáŋ** or **šamná** in others. Use whatever is more common in your local area.
Note 4: The word **tȟó** is also used to express the green color of grass and leaves. This will be more thoroughly explained in a later unit. Feel free to tell the children in case they ask or it becomes an issue.
Note 5: Albert White Hat uses **zítȟo** instead of **tȟózi** for "green". And so this may be the usage on Rosebud. Use your local variant.
Note 6: Some speakers stress the compounded colors on the first syllable others on the second (e.g. **zíša** instead of **zišá**).

šá	zíša	tȟó	tȟózi
šastáŋ	tȟósaŋ	zí	ǧí
ská	sáŋ	ȟóta	sápa

Lé **wígmuŋke** héčha.

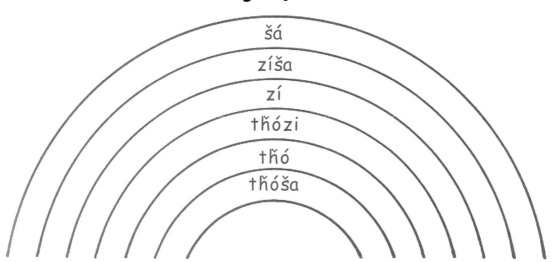

šá

zíša

zí

tȟózi

tȟó

tȟóša

Lé wówapi tȟó.

Lé šúŋka ǧí.

Lé kimímela zí.

Lé igmú sápe.

Lé wíyatke šá.

Lé wakšíča ská.

Lé čȟaŋbláska ȟóta.

Lé gnaška tȟózi.

Lé wóžuha tȟósape.

22

5. Háŋ naíŋš hiyá?

5. Háŋ naíŋš hiyá?   Yes or no?

Šúŋka kiŋ ǧí hwo/he?	Háŋ	Hiyá
Wóžuha kiŋ zí he?	Háŋ	Hiyá
Wíyatke kiŋ tȟó he?	Háŋ	Hiyá
Kimímela kiŋ šá he?	Háŋ	Hiyá
Igmú kiŋ ská he?	Háŋ	Hiyá
Gnaška kiŋ sáŋ he?	Háŋ	Hiyá

6. Color by number.

wanǧí = šá

tópa = tȟósaŋ

šakówiŋ = ǧí

wikčémna = zí

núŋpa = ská

šákpe = šastáŋ

yámni = tȟósapa

záptaŋ = ȟóta

napčíyuŋka = tȟózi

šaglóǧaŋ = tȟóša

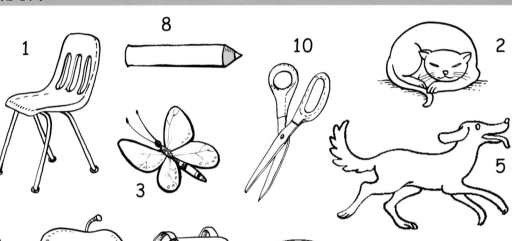

7. Oówa kiŋ owá po/pe!   Name the colors!

šá	zí	tȟó	ǧí	sápa	ská	ȟóta
sáŋ	zíša	šastáŋ	tȟózi	tȟósapa	tȟósaŋ	tȟóša

23

5. Lé tókheča hwo/he? What does it look like?

miméla **miméla** **oblótȟuŋ** **oblótȟuŋ**
čík'ala tȟáŋka čík'ala tȟáŋka

oíse-yámni **oíse-yámni** **oblótȟuŋ-háŋska** **oblótȟuŋ-háŋska**
čík'ala tȟáŋka čík'ala tȟáŋka

wičháȟpi **wičháȟpi** **pȟéstola** **pȟéstola**
čík'ala tȟáŋka čík'ala tȟáŋka

ičázopi háŋska **ičázopi** ptéčela

1. Tóna hwo/he? Count the number of shapes you see!

miméla _____**tópa**_____

wičháȟpi _____

oblótȟuŋ _____

oblótȟuŋ háŋska _____

ičázopi _____

oíse-yámni _____

pȟéstola _____

24

Vocabulary on pg. 103
Sounds: kȟ and kh (for instructions cf. p. 97)

Have ready the flashcards of geometric shapes in different colors and sizes.

Geometric Shapes

Geometric shapes are important in Lakota culture. They have always been used as symbols for natural features in traditional artwork. Therefore, it is important for children to learn to recognize the various shapes and name them in Lakota.

Children enjoy activities with colored shapes cut out of paper. This unit offers many flexible options and activities which help build the vocabulary of numbers, colors, and sizes.

1. Begin the unit by teaching words for geometric shapes. Use the flashcard activities (cf. p. 90–93).
2. Try the following activities after you are certain that the children know the shape vocabulary. With flashcards or two objects of different size, demonstrate the difference between tȟáŋka {big} and čík'ala {small}. Put two flashcards on the board, e.g. small dog and big dog. Then write and say the two words (tȟáŋka, čík'ala).
3. Start working with the Lesson Page of this unit. Ask the children to point at the shape that you name. Say e.g.: miméla tȟáŋka, oblótȟuŋ čík'ala, oíse-yámni čík'ala, oblótȟuŋ-háŋska tȟáŋka. The children point at the proper shape.
4. Ask the children to point at the shape that has the color you name, as in: sápa, šá, sáŋ, tȟóša etc. Finally, ask the children to say the color of the object that you name. E.g. miméla čík'ala ➔ šá; etc.

Break

Let children relax by coloring objects in the exercises one and two on the following page. Help them understand the written instructions if they can't read. Alternatively, use the two exercises as a review at the beginning of the next class.

Review of Háŋ and Hiyá

Later, do a flashcard activity involving shapes with which you review the words Háŋ and Hiyá, and the question Lé miméla (héčha) hwo/he?. Children answer with Háŋ or Hiyá.

Review of Numbers

Prepare 10–12 flashcards with different geometric shapes in both large and small versions and in different colors. Put the cards on the board and number them (1 to 10 or 1 to 12).
1. Name individual shapes. The children should say the numbers, like:
    oblótȟuŋ tȟáŋka ➔ tópa; miméla tȟó ➔ wikčémna
2. Say the numbers. The children name the shapes, e.g.:
    núŋpa ➔ oíse-yámni; záptaŋ ➔ ičázopi
3. Say the numbers. The children say the sizes, e.g.
    waŋží ➔ tȟáŋka; napčíyuŋka ➔ čík'ala

Colors in the Inanimate Plural

This is the first time children are introduced to the inanimate plurals of the colors (i.e. their reduplicated forms). Avoid using the plural for animate items (e.g. animals). This is introduced later in Unit 15 (page 60).

Choose flashcards of geometrical shapes. Ideally choose those with multiple shapes of the same type and color on one card. With their help, demonstrate the plural forms of colors; make sure to start with the basic color terms, i.e. those that don't combine two colors (šá, tȟó, ská, sáŋ, zí, ǧí, ȟóta, sápa):

• Show a flashcard (e.g. with three red squares) and say: Lená šašá. Continue with other shapes until all the colors are used.

• Show the same flashcards one by one and ask the children to say the colors in the plural.

• Do the same activity with compound color terms (tȟózi, tȟóša, tȟósaŋ, tȟósapa, zíša) without reduplicating them.

Prepare labels with singular and plural forms of color terms. Make two columns on the board, one with header "One" (or waŋží) the other with "Many" (or óta). Then ask the children to put the labels in the proper column keeping the singular and plural forms on the same line.

The children can practice the plural forms further in exercises 5 and 6 on the next page (provide help to non-reading students).

Ask the children if they are able to explain to you which of the color-words are doubled and which are not.

Demonstrate the verb bluhá {I have}:

Hold up an object (or a picture) and say, e.g.: Oblótȟuŋ waŋ bluhá. {I have a square.}

Repeat this several times and then ask children to hold something up. Ask them this:

Táku (čha) luhá hwo/he? {What do you have?}

Once you are sure the children know the meaning of bluhá and luhá, let them hold similar conversations in pairs. With more advanced students use more complex sentences, e.g.: Oblótȟuŋ zizí tópa bluhá.

In the next class, review bluhá and luhá. With more advanced students, demonstrate yuhá {he/she has}. Ask about individual students in ways like: Robert táku (čha) yuhá hwo/he? {What does Robert have?}

Note 1: A variant of the word oblótȟuŋ {square} is oblétȟuŋ. Use and teach whichever variant is more common in your local area. Deloria gives "obló" as the root of the word. Many speakers (especially in Medicine Root District and in Cheyenne River) refer to obló-yámni as the word for triangle.

Note 2: The five-point star was preferred by the reviewers because of its common use today. Traditionally, four point stars were used as well as stars of unspecified number of points.

Note 3: The word ičázopi {line} implies that the line was made with a pen or pencil, while ičáǧopi would be a line made with a stick in sand or carved in wood.

2. Yawápi na owá po/pe! Read And Color!

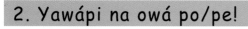

oíse-yámni	oblótȟuŋ	pȟéstola	miméla	oblótȟuŋ-háŋska

wičháȟpi

ičázopi

 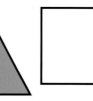 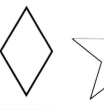 

3. Read or listen to your teacher and then color the shapes:

1. **Miméla** <u>tȟáŋka</u> kiŋ zíša.

2. **Miméla** <u>číkʼala</u> kiŋ tȟó.

3. **Oblótȟuŋ** <u>tȟáŋka</u> kiŋ tȟózi.

4. **Oblótȟuŋ** <u>číkʼala</u> kiŋ tȟóša.

5. **Oblótȟuŋ-háŋska** kiŋ tȟósaŋ.

6. **Oíse-yámni** <u>tȟáŋka</u> kiŋ ǧí.

7. **Oíse-yámni** <u>číkʼala</u> kiŋ zí.

8. **Ičázo** <u>ptéčela</u> kiŋ sápe.

9. **Ičázo** <u>háŋska</u> kiŋ ȟóta.

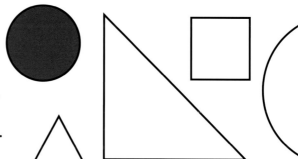

4. The numbers reveal the colors.

waŋží	núŋpa	yámni	tópa	záptaŋ	šákpe	šakówiŋ	šaglóǧaŋ

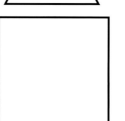

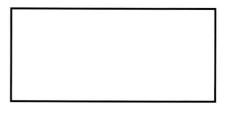

26

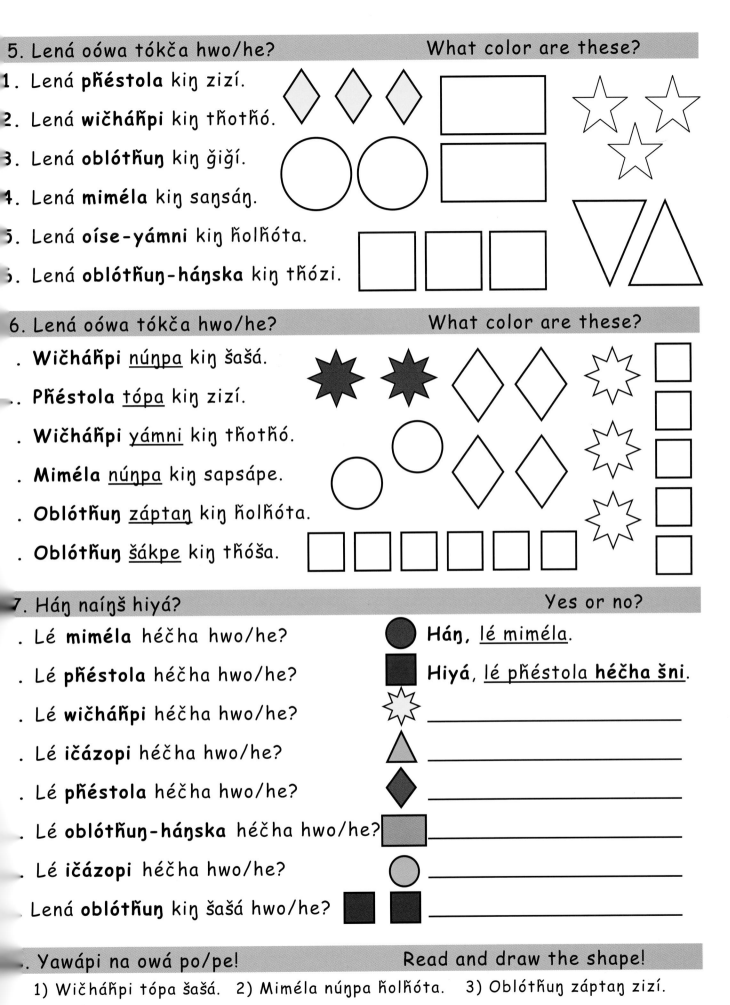

5. Lená oówa tókča hwo/he? — What color are these?

1. Lená **pȟéstola** kiŋ zizí.
2. Lená **wičháȟpi** kiŋ tȟotȟó.
3. Lená **oblótȟuŋ** kiŋ ǧiǧí.
4. Lená **miméla** kiŋ saŋsáŋ.
5. Lená **oíse-yámni** kiŋ ȟolȟóta.
6. Lená **oblótȟuŋ-háŋska** kiŋ tȟózi.

6. Lená oówa tókča hwo/he? — What color are these?

. **Wičháȟpi** <u>núŋpa</u> kiŋ šašá.
. **Pȟéstola** <u>tópa</u> kiŋ zizí.
. **Wičháȟpi** <u>yámni</u> kiŋ tȟotȟó.
. **Miméla** <u>núŋpa</u> kiŋ sapsápe.
. **Oblótȟuŋ** <u>záptaŋ</u> kiŋ ȟolȟóta.
. **Oblótȟuŋ** <u>šákpe</u> kiŋ tȟóša.

7. Háŋ naíŋš hiyá? — Yes or no?

. Lé **miméla** héčha hwo/he? — Háŋ, <u>lé miméla</u>.
. Lé **pȟéstola** héčha hwo/he? — Hiyá, <u>lé pȟéstola</u> **héčha šni**.
. Lé **wičháȟpi** héčha hwo/he? _____
. Lé **ičázopi** héčha hwo/he? _____
. Lé **pȟéstola** héčha hwo/he? _____
. Lé **oblótȟuŋ-háŋska** héčha hwo/he? _____
. Lé **ičázopi** héčha hwo/he? _____
. Lená **oblótȟuŋ** kiŋ šašá hwo/he? _____

. Yawápi na owá po/pe! — Read and draw the shape!

1) Wičháȟpi tópa šašá. 2) Miméla núŋpa ȟolȟóta. 3) Oblótȟuŋ záptaŋ zizí.

kiŋyékhiyapi

šúŋkawakȟáŋ

wáta

Táku luhá he?

šúŋka   haŋpóšpu   hunúŋp nagmíyaŋpi

igmú

tȟaté kaȟwógyapi

matȟó

hokšípaslohe

Iyéčhiŋkyaŋke waŋ bluhá.

iyók'iŋpa

thiíkčeya   tȟápa   čhéǧa

iyéčhiŋkyaŋke

thípi

oyáte itȟókšu

iwátȟókšu   owayawa itȟókšu   ȟemáni

Vocabulary on pg. **104**.
Sounds: **tȟ, th** (instructions cf. p. **98**).

In order for children to enjoy learning and using a language they need to be able to talk about things they like. Toys are as important to children today as they were long ago.

Before you start this lesson unit ask the children to look at the Lesson Page. Ask them if they have any of the toys in the picture at home. The children should tell you which they have and you will ask them to bring one of their toys to the next class. You may want to make sure that no one brings their bicycle or that too many bring the same thing. For the following activities it helps to have a variety of toys.

Allowing children to use their own toys stimulates learning activity by creating a real-life situation. In case children cannot bring their toys, use flashcards of the toys instead for the same activities.

- Ask the children (one at a time) to hold up their toy and to ask you something like:
  Student: **Lé táku hwo/he?**
  Teacher: **Lé iyéchiŋkyaŋke héčha.**
  Each child repeats after the teacher (**Eyá yo!**).

- Hold up a toy and demonstrate the following sentence:
  Iyéchiŋkyaŋke waŋ bluhá. {I have a car.}
  Help the children to say the same sentence about their toys. With the youngest children, be happy even if they say only the name of the toy.
  If you feel that your students managed the sentence structure, encourage the use of gender endings (**yeló** or **kštó/ye**) after **bluhá**.

- Then ask individual children something like:
  Robert, táku (čha) luhá hwo/he?
  {Robert, what do you have?}
  Each child answers like:
  Šúŋkawakȟáŋ waŋ bluhá. {I have a horse.} or
  Šúŋkawakȟáŋ čha bluhá. {A horse is what I have.}
  Don't be disappointed if some children give you only the term for the toy and praise them in any case. They may also omit the indefinite article (**waŋ**).

- Tell the children to ask each other about their toys:
  Táku (čha) luhá hwo/he? {What do you have?} ➜
  Matȟó (waŋ bluhá) (yeló/kštó). {(I have a) bear.}

You may also want to add color to the sentence later. Demonstrate this by taking a toy into your hands and saying: **Iyéchiŋkyaŋke tȟó waŋ bluhá.** {I have a blue car.}

- Try this activity: Ask the children to sit or stand in a circle and to try to memorize what toys the other children have. Then have the children put the toys behind their backs (or put them away). Ask the children to try to remember and name somebody else's toy (without naming the person sitting next to them). For example:

  David iwátȟokšu waŋ yuhá. {David has a truck.}
  (With advanced students: **David iwátȟokšu sápa waŋ yuhá**. {David has a <u>black</u> truck.})

Whenever a child makes a correct guess, he or she exchanges his/her place with the child being guessed or receives a point/picture/sticker.

Workbook Pages

Use the coloring exercises on the following pages to give the small children a break. If appropriate, you can also use the colored images for additional exercises. The children can, for instance, describe the colors of their pictures: **Šúŋka sápa waŋ bluhá.** {I have a black dog.}

You can adapt many of the flashcard activities on page 90 to be used with the toys.

With older or more advanced students introduce **mitȟáwa, nitȟáwa, tȟáwa**, e.g.:
  Iyéchiŋkyaŋke mitȟáwa kiŋ tȟó. {My car is blue.}
  or
  Iyéchiŋkiŋyaŋke (tȟó) kiŋ mitȟáwa. {The (blue) car is mine.}
  Make sure to review **bluhá, luhá** and **yuhá** in every class of this lesson, using one of the short activities above.

Note 1: Some of the toy words, such as "teddy bear", "toy car" etc. would normally be modified with **hokšíčala**, e.g.: **matȟó hokšíčala** {teddy bear}. For purposes of teaching new vocabulary and sentences, we recommend using the shorter terms. Children will learn the proper terms later.
Note 2: Variations for "doll" are **haŋpóšpu hokšíčala, hopóšpu**, and **hokšíčala káǧapi**.

1.   Can you color these?

iyéčhiŋkyaŋke, iwátȟokšu, kiŋyékhiyapi, oyáte itȟókšu, owáyawa itȟókšu, thiíkčeya, tȟápa, čhéǧa, hokšípaslohe, iyók'iŋpa, thípi, wáta.

2. Do you know their names?

matȟó, hunúŋp nagmíyaŋpi, ȟemáni, tȟaté kaȟwógyapi, šúŋka, igmú, haŋpóšpu, šúŋkawakȟáŋ

Look at the pictures! How did children dress long ago? What are the Lakota names for the modern and traditional pieces of clothing?

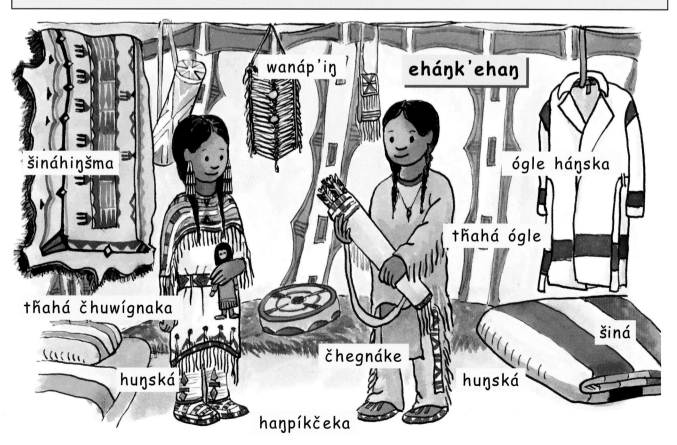

Vocabulary on pg. 104.
Sounds: pȟ, ph (instructions cf. p 98)

Use flashcard activities to introduce new vocabulary (cf. pages 90–93).
To begin, teach only the modern clothing and introduce the traditional clothes only in higher grades. The K-3 students can recognize them passively, but should not be required to know them.

After the flashcard activities have been used to reinforce the new vocabulary, review the colors in this way:
Teacher: **Ógle kiŋ lé oówa tókča hwo/he?**
Student: **Tȟózi.**
Teacher: **Uŋzóǧe kiŋ lé oówa tókča hwo/he?**
Student: **Tȟó.**

Afterwards, reverse the dialogue:
Children should say the clothing items and you tell them the color. This can also be done in pairs.

Later, ask the children to close their books and look around (ideally they should be seated in a circle). Then make a statement such as:
Ógle zí makípazo wo! {Show me a yellow shirt.}
Háŋpa tȟotȟó makípazo wo! {Show me blue shoes.}

The children should point at a classmate who is wearing the mentioned item of clothing.

Introduce the verb úŋ {to wear}
After the children are familiar with the new vocabulary, introduce the verb **úŋ** {to wear}. You can do it like this. Take your jacket and say:
Lé ógle šókela héčha.
Then, put it on and say:
Ógle šókela múŋ.
Name some other things that you are wearing, e.g.:
Uŋzóǧe sápa múŋ. Ógle šá múŋ. etc.

Then ask individual children what they are wearing:
Teacher: **Táku (čha) núŋ he?** {What are you wearing?} **Student**: **Uŋzóǧe tȟó múŋ.** {I am wearing blue pants.}
Then ask the children to do the same activity in pairs.
When the children become familiar with the verb forms **múŋ** {I wear} and **núŋ** {you wear}, you can introduce **úŋ** {he/she wears}. As an exercise, let them choose one of their classmates and describe what he or she is wearing.

Review of inanimate plural:
With paired clothing items, such as shoes, socks and gloves, you can review the inanimate plural of colors.
For instance:

Háŋpa ǧiǧí bluhá.
Huŋyákȟuŋ ȟolȟóta bluhá.
Napíŋkpa sapsápa bluhá.
Demonstrate the sentences first and then help the students repeat them about their own clothes.

Play "Who is it?"
Tell the children that you are going to think of someone in the class and they must guess who it is. They need to ask questions such as: **Ógle zí úŋ hwo/he?** {Is he/she wearing a yellow shirt?}, **Uŋzóǧe sápa úŋ hwo/he?** {Is he/she wearing black pants?} etc.

Mitȟáwa, kiŋ
With the upper grades or more advanced classes you may introduce (or review) the following sentence structure:
Ógle nitȟáwa kiŋ oówa tókča hwo/he? {What color is your shirt?}
Ógle mitȟáwa kiŋ sápe. {My shirt is black.}
Háŋpa nitȟáwa kiŋ oówa tókča hwo/he? {What color are your shoes?}
Háŋpa mitȟáwa kiŋ tȟotȟó. {My shoes are blue.}

New versus Old
You can also introduce the adjectives **lečhála** {new} and **tȟaŋníla** {old}. Both are used only with inanimate objects. You can practice these two words in sentences such as:
Uŋzóǧe mitȟáwa kiŋ tȟaŋníla. {My pants are old.}
Nitéhepi mitȟáwa kiŋ lečhála. {My skirt is new.}
Háŋpa mitȟáwa kiŋ tȟaŋnígnila. {My shoes are old.}
Háŋpa mitȟáwa kiŋ lečhákčhala. {My shoes are new.}

Note 1: In Pine Ridge **lečhála** is commonly used for "new" and **tȟéča** for "young", while in Cheyenne River **tȟéča** seems to be used in both senses.
Note 2: **Uŋzóǧiŋ** is another form of **uŋzóǧe** {pants}.
Note 3: The word **nitéhepi** {skirt} is only recognized in some communities. If your local variant is different, introduce that word in your classes. **Nitéhepi** is given by Riggs in his Dakota dictionary and later by Buechel in his Lakota dictionary (indicated as an old word by White Rabbit) and by Deloria some 10 years later. She also provided the word **uŋpí** {skirt, petticoat}. **Nitéhepi** is probably in use on the Rosebud and the Cheyenne River reservations as indicated in books by Albert White Hat and David Little Elk.
Note 4: The word for jacket is both **ógle šóka** and **ógle šókela**.
Note 5: Other terms for "neck-scarf" are **tȟahú iyákpehaŋpi** and **tȟahú iyápehe**. **Watȟéšlaka** is given for "head-scarf".
Note 6: The generic term for moccasins is **haŋpíkčeka**. Beaded moccasins are called **haŋpíkčeka kšúpi** or **háŋpakšupi**. **Wanápʼiŋ** is any necklace, while **huhú wanápʼiŋ** is specifically the one in the picture (one reviewer gave **wawóslata wanápʼiŋ**).

ógle   nitéhepi   háŋpa   ógle zibzípela   čhuwígnaka   mahél úŋpi

uŋzóǧe   iphíyake   huŋyákȟuŋ   napíŋkpa   ógle šóka   wapȟóštaŋla

Linda emáčiyapi. Lená múŋ kštó: Ógle zigzíča zí. Nitéhepi tȟósape. Huŋyákȟuŋ skaská. Háŋpa tȟotȟó.

Elisabeth emáčiyapi.
Lená múŋ kštó:
Ógle zigzíča šastáŋ.
Nitéhepi tȟósaŋ.
Huŋyákȟuŋ šašá.
Háŋpa sapsápe.

Háu. Elmer emáčiyapi.
Ógle mitȟáwa kiŋ tȟózi.
Uŋzóǧe mitȟáwa kiŋ tȟó.
Háŋpa mitȟáwa kiŋ ǧiǧí.

Háu, toníktuka hwo?
Robert emáčiyapi.
Lená múŋ weló: Ógle
tȟózi. Uŋzóǧe tȟó.
Háŋpa ǧiǧí.

Can you write or say in Lakota what you are wearing?

35

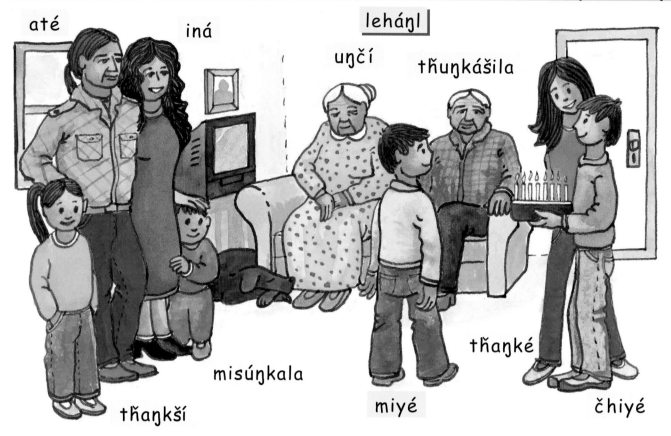

Do boys use the same terms as girls to name their relatives? Which are different? Which are the same? What do they mean? Study the pictures to find out.

Vocabulary on pg. 104.

Sounds: č, čh (instructions on pg. 99).

The Lesson Page shows the kinship terms used by a boy (in the picture of a contemporary family) and those used by a girl (in the picture of a pre-reservation family). Teachers may want to explain to the children that the kinship terms in the two pictures are not different because of the different time periods, but because they are used by a boy and a girl.

Teachers may also explain to the children that members of a family preferably address each other with kinship terms rather than personal names. Names are more often used for reference than for address.

The labels in the pictures provide the terms of address. The terms misúŋkala {younger brother} and mitȟáŋkala {woman's younger sister} include the notion of "my" (mi-).

Teach the kinship terms

Point at a character in the picture and then say the appropriate kinship term. Children repeat. Then play the audio CD and children should point at the characters in their books.

You can also use the picture of the contemporary Lakota family to review some clothing terms. Ask about the characters in the picture and the children should respond with the proper kinship term such as:

Teacher: Tuwá ógle šá úŋ hwo/he?
Children: Tȟuŋkášila.

Ask the children to draw a picture of their family on a sheet of paper. They should draw their parents, grandparents and siblings. Ask the children to write the names of their relatives on the picture (This should be done with sensitivity for the children who don't live with their families).

"My-" forms of kinship terms

Introduce the "my-" reference construction by giving the example of "my father": até-waye kiŋ (-waye kiŋ is appended to the kinship term). Then ask the children to create the "my-" forms of the relatives you name:

Teacher: iná ➜ Students: iná-waye kiŋ etc.
The terms are:
ináwaye kiŋ {my mother}; atéwaye kiŋ {my father}; uŋčíwaye {my grandmother}; tȟuŋkášilawaye kiŋ {my grandfather}; čiyéwaye kiŋ {my older brother (man speaking)}; thiblówaye {my older brother (woman speaking)}; tȟaŋkéwaye kiŋ {my older sister (man speaking)}; čhuwéwaye kiŋ {my older sister (woman speaking)}; tȟaŋkšíwaye kiŋ {my younger sister (man speaking)}; suŋkáwaye kiŋ {my younger brother}; tȟaŋkáwaye {my younger sister (woman speaking)}; čhiŋkšíwaye kiŋ {my son}; čhuŋkšíwaye kiŋ {my daughter}.

Make the children aware of the two exceptions to the rule:
misúŋkala -> suŋká-waye kiŋ {my younger brother}
mitȟáŋkala -> tȟaŋkáwaye kiŋ {my younger sister}

With students who read, write some of the terms on the board. Read them and then ask the children if they can find

out how to say "my mother" or "my father". To make it clearer to the students you can use a hyphen: iná-waye kiŋ. This should make it easier for the children to see where the "my" part stands. (See the explanation of slow and fast pronunciation of -waye kiŋ on page 101). It should be made clear that this construction can be used only with kinship terms; remind them of mitȟáwa which is used for things. A more thorough explanation of the –ye kiŋ form is covered in Level 2.

- **Talk about your family**

Using their family pictures, have them describe their family in a way like: Iná-waye kiŋ Mary ečíyapi. Até-waye kiŋ Bob ečíyapi. etc.

- čhiŋkší and čhuŋkší: Introduce and practice the terms čhiŋkší {son} and čhuŋkší {daughter}.

Optional: With more advanced students, introduce the 3rd person singular forms of reference (i.e. his/her ….). They are: húŋku {his/her mother}; atkúku {his/her father}; kȟúŋšitku {his/her grandmother}; tȟuŋkášitku {his/her grandfather}; čhiyéku {his older brother}; thiblóku {her older brother}; tȟaŋkéku {his older sister}; čhuwéku {her older sister}; tȟaŋkšitku {his younger sister}; suŋkáku {his/her younger brother}; tȟaŋkáku {her younger sister}; čhiŋkšitku {his/her son}; čhuŋkšítku {his/her daughter}.

- You can also add the -yaye kiŋ form for "your [kinship term]". Your students can practice this construction in a dialogue such as:
1) Robert: Iná-yaye kiŋ táku ečíyapi hwo/he?
2) David: Iná-waye kiŋ Mary ečíyapi.
3) Robert: David húŋku Mary ečíyapi.

- Ask the children: "What do you call me if I address you like this?":
Teacher: Thibló. {Older brother (woman speaking)}
Student: Tȟaŋkší. {Younger sister (man speaking)}
This is a complex activity and should only be used with more advanced students.

The exercises on the second workbook page will also require a teacher's assistance.

Note 1: The other kinship terms, such as: aunt, uncle, cousins, etc. are introduced in Level 2.

Note 2: Tȟuŋkášila is a formal term of address. Informally, children call their grandfathers kaká (among the Oglála and Sičháŋǧu) or lalá (in the northern Lakota communities). Teachers should introduce these terms as well (including kaká-waye kiŋ / lalá-waye kiŋ for "my grandfather").

Note 3: Most communities use uŋčí as the only or generic term for "grandmother". Some communities, however, use uŋčí for the maternal grandmother and kȟuŋší for the paternal grandmother.

Note 4: Mitȟáŋkala and misúŋkala are often shortened to mitȟáŋ and misúŋ.

How do they address each other? Do you know where to put these words?
thibló, tȟaŋké, čhuwé, mitȟáŋkala, tȟaŋkší, uŋčí, tȟuŋkášila, misúŋkala, čhiyé, até, iná

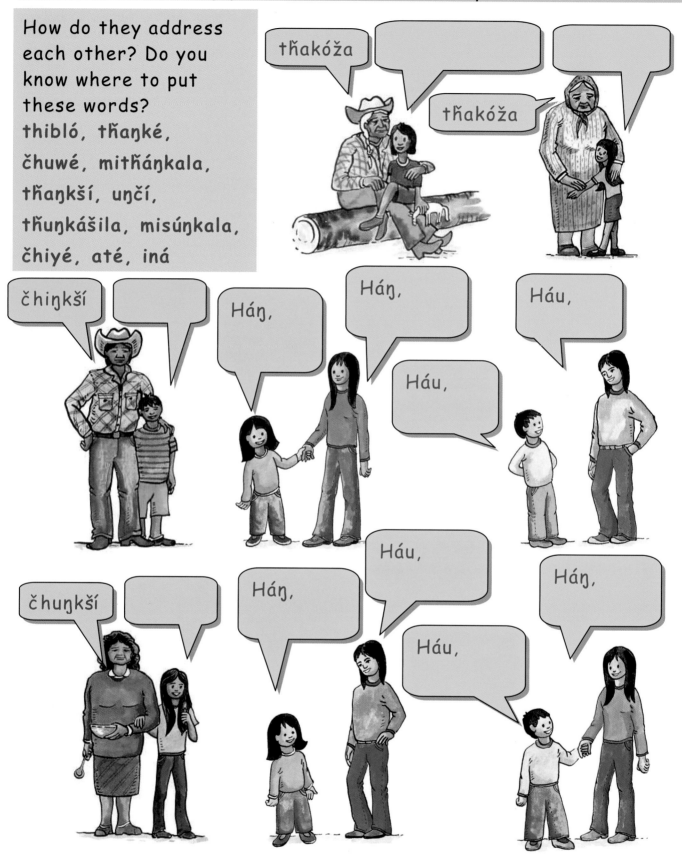

tȟakóža

tȟakóža

čhiŋkší

Háŋ,

Háŋ,

Háu,

Háu,

čhuŋkší

Háŋ,

Háu,

Háu,

Háŋ,

Draw a picture of your family. Then label each person in Lakota.

38

3. Táku ewíčhakiyapi hwo/he?   What are their names?

Até-waye kiŋ <u>Bill</u> ečíyapi. Iná-waye kiŋ <u>Lisa</u> ečíyapi. Suŋká-waye kiŋ <u>John</u> ečíyapi. Tȟaŋkší-waye kiŋ <u>Deb</u> ečíyapi. Čhiyé-waye kiŋ <u>Bob</u> ečíyapi. Tȟaŋké-waye kiŋ <u>Vivian</u> ečíyapi. Na **míš** <u>Wilmer</u> emáčiyapi.

4. Táku ewíčhakiyapi hwo/he?   What are their names?

Até-waye kiŋ <u>John</u> ečíyapi. Iná-waye kiŋ <u>Mary</u> ečíyapi. Tȟuŋkášila-waye kiŋ <u>Leonard</u> ečíyapi. Uŋčí-waye kiŋ <u>Ann</u> ečíyapi. Čhuwé-waye kiŋ Sophia ečíyapi. Suŋká-waye kiŋ <u>Ron</u> ečíyapi. Thibló-waye kiŋ <u>Elmer</u> ečíyapi. Tȟaŋká-waye kiŋ <u>Verola</u> ečíyapi. Na **míš** <u>Tina</u> emáčiyapi.

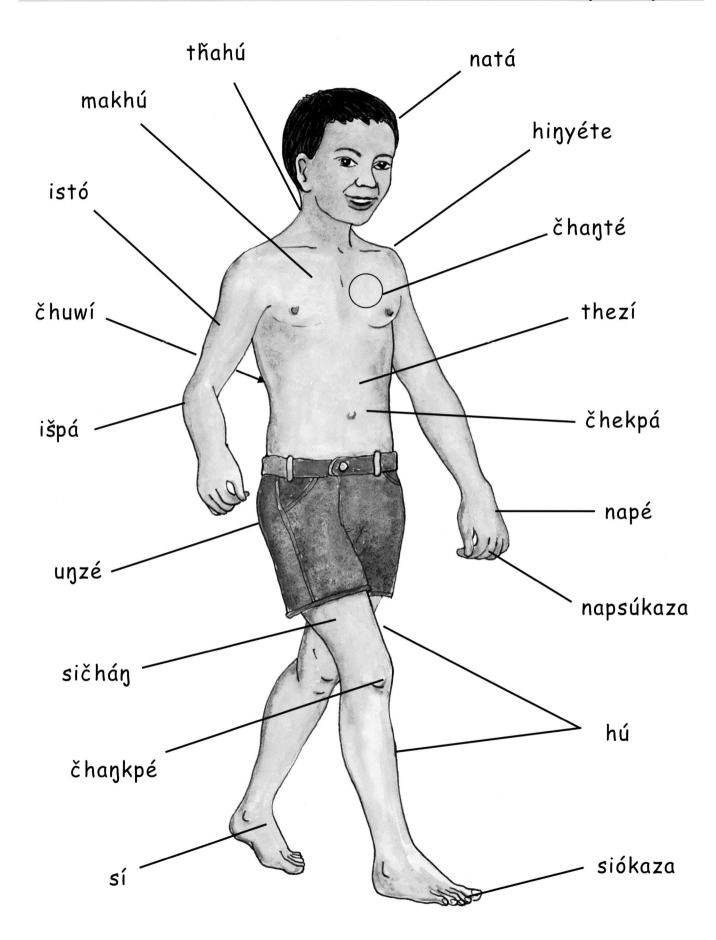

tȟahú

natá

makhú

hiŋyéte

istó

čhaŋté

thezí

čhuwí

čhekpá

išpá

napé

uŋzé

napsúkaza

sičháŋ

hú

čhaŋkpé

sí

siókaza

Vocabulary on pg. 104.
Sounds: **s**, **š** and **z**, **ž** (for instructions cf. pg. 99).

Children usually enjoy learning body part terms. There are many fun activities they can do while learning them.

The vocabulary in this unit is introduced and practiced through activities involving the children's own bodies. If teachers want extra material they can make their own handout activities, such as having the children match words with a picture of a person.

There are eighteen body parts in this unit. Introduce them to the children in two groups:

1) **natá, thezí, napé, čhaŋté, čhuwí, istó, sí, hú, tȟahú**

2) **makȟú, čhekpá, išpá, napsúkaza, siókaza, čhaŋkpé, uŋzé, hiŋyéte, sičháŋ**

The second group should be introduced after the children are thoroughly familiar with the first group.

- Touch your arm with your hand and say **istó**. Ask the children to do the same and repeat the word after you. Continue with other words from the first group. Alternatively, use the audio CD to demonstrate by touching while you listen. Explain that **čhaŋté** means "heart" as it may not be obvious just by touching the left side of your chest.

After you feel that the children know the words, reinforce the words through the following activity:

- Ask the children to touch the body part you name. Then say: **Natá églutȟaŋ po!** {Touch your heads!}. **Sí églutȟaŋ po!** {Touch your feet!} etc.
- Then ask the children to name the body part that you touch.

Do the same sequence of activities for the second group of body parts.

- **Play the game Simon heyé:**

Children touch the named body part only if **Simon heyé** {Simon Says} is used. For instance:

Simon heyé: Natá églutȟaŋ po! [The children touch.]
Simon heyé: Sí églutȟaŋ po! [The children touch.]
Čhuwí églutȟaŋ po! [The children don't touch.]

- **With more advanced classes teach these sentences**:

Sí núŋpa mayúkȟe. {I have two feet.}
Napé núŋpa mayúkȟe. {I have two hands.}
Natá waŋžíla mayúkȟe. {I have only one head.} etc.

Ideally, the children should repeat these sentences after you while also pointing at the mentioned body part(s).

- **How many?**

Ask the children to say the number of a body part you name, e.g.:

čhuwí ➔ waŋží; natá ➔ waŋží, hú ➔ núŋpa, čhekpá ➔ waŋží; istó ➔ núŋpa, išpá ➔ núŋpa, napsúkaza ➔ wikčémna, etc.

- **How many legs?**

Name various animals, creatures or even things and ask the children to respond with the appropriate number of legs, e.g.:

hokšíla ➔ núŋpa; šúŋka ➔ tópa; waŋblí ➔ núŋpa; iktómi ➔ šaglóǧaŋ; wablúška ➔ šákpe; oákaŋke ➔ tópa; akáŋwowapi ➔ tópa etc.

- **Play with Rhymes**

Children love rhymes and songs. They are enjoyable and help with word memorization and sentence structures.

Most of the body parts have at least one rhyming companion. Therefore you can play a game with the children like this:

Tell them that you will say a body part. They must respond with one that rhymes and at the same time touch the body part they name. Demonstrate: **thezí ↔ čhuwí**.

Here are the pairs: **išpá ↔ čhekpá (+ natá); tȟahú ↔ makȟú (hú); thezí ↔ čhuwí (+ sí); napé ↔ čhaŋkpé (+ uŋzé); napsúkaza ↔ siókaza**. There are no rhymes for **istó** and **sičháŋ**.

You can also use the favorite song "Head, Shoulders, Knees and Toes" in Lakota.

With advanced students introduce (demonstrate) possessive pronouns: for 1st person singular the prefix **ma-** or **mi-** is used (**manáta** {my head}, **minápe** {my hand}), for 2nd person singular prefix **ni-** is used (**nisí** {your foot}).

With older students make sure to explain that **mitȟáwa/nitȟáwa/tȟáwa** are not used with body parts.

Independent personal pronouns (like **mitȟáwa**) are not used with body parts (and kinship terms). This is one of the most common errors students make when translating from English to Lakota.

Furthermore, in sentences like, "My nose is big," possessive pronouns aren't used at all. Instead, the information is carried in the verb, as in:

"My nose is big." = **Pȟasú matȟáŋka.** {nose – I am big.}

- The "Touch your … " game is very good when a change in activity is needed.

Note 1: **Hiŋyéte** is sometimes used as the generic term for "shoulder". Its meaning refers to the back part of the shoulder. Other anatomical terms for this area are: shoulder joint – **abló**, the upper arm – **aȟčó**, and the forearm – **istó**. **Istó** is also used as a generic word for the entire arm. **Note 2**: Many reviewers gave **sipȟá** as the variant for "toes", while some referred to it as the "big toe" only. **Note 3**: Variants for "fingers" are: **napsúkaza, napsúokaza, napsúkazuŋte** and **napsú**. **Note 4**: All reviewers except two stated that **uŋzé** {buttocks} has no derogatory connotation in Lakota language.

Lená <u>waskúyeča</u> héčha:

tȟaspáŋ

tȟaspáŋ zí

tȟaspáŋ pȟéstola

čhaŋpȟá

wičhágnaška

kȟáŋta

wagmúšpaŋšni

zíškopela

wažúšteča

Zíškopela yačhíŋ he?

Hiyá, zíškopa waštéwalake šni.

čhuŋwíyapehe

Tȟaspáŋ waštéwalake ló.

Lená <u>watȟótȟo</u> héčha:

waȟpé iŋkpážiži

tȟíŋpsiŋla

kuŋkúŋ

pšíŋ

uŋžíŋžiŋtka

bló

pȟaŋǧí zizí

Vocabulary on pg. 105.
Sounds: h, w, y, l, m, n (cf. pg. 99).

First, teach new words by using various flashcard activities (cf. pages 90–93). Teach the fruits first. After several flashcard activities you can let the children color the outlined images on the following workbook page. Then do some other flashcard activities. With second graders you can let the children match the words to the pictures (on the next page). After you are sure that the students are familiar with fruits, start introducing vegetables with the same strategy.

• Waskúyeča naíŋš Watȟótȟo {Fruit or Vegetable}

Put a flashcard with an apple on the blackboard and write **waskúyeča** above it. Then say: **Tȟaspáŋ kiŋ waskúyeča héčha.** {Apple is a fruit.}

Then put a flashcard of potatoes on the blackboard, write **watȟótȟo** above it and say **Bló kiŋ watȟótȟo héčha.** {Potato is a vegetable}.

Then ask the children to match the other flashcards with one of the two groups. You may want to make sure that the children understand the words **waskúyeča** and **watȟótȟo** before they start matching other cards. Individual children come, take a flashcard, and add it to one of the groups.

After all the flashcards are divided between the two groups, the teacher names a fruit or vegetable, the children respond with **waskúyeča** or **watȟótȟo**.

This activity can be used for review in the next class, this time without the pictures.

• Review Inanimate Plural of Colors

Show the children a flashcard of a banana and ask: **Zíškopela kiŋ lé oówa tókča hwo/he?** {What color is the banana?}. The children respond with: **(Zíškopela kiŋ) zí.** Show the picture of strawberries and ask: **Wažúšteča kiŋ lená oówa tókča hwo/he?** {What color are the strawberries?} Children respond with: **(Wažúšteča kiŋ lená) šašá.** or **Lená šašá**.

Continue with the plural constructions of other fruits and vegetables. This way the children review the inanimate plural of colors (reduplicated forms).

You may also practice with sentences like this: **Zíškopela kiŋ (lená) zizí.** {Bananas are yellow.} **Uŋžíŋžiŋtka kiŋ (lená) šašá.** {Tomatoes are red.} **Bló kiŋ (lená) ǧiǧí.** {Potatoes are brown.}

• Wašté naíŋš šíča

Write **wašté** and **šíča** on the board, say those words and ask the children if they know what they mean. They will be familiar with **wašté**. Give them a hint about **šíča** by saying it is the opposite of **wašté**. The students repeat the words after you.

Demonstrate this activity. The teacher names (or shows a picture of) a fruit/vegetable, individual children respond with **wašté** or **šíča** according to their likes and dislikes. Children can do this either in pairs or groups, or by standing in a circle taking turns in naming the fruits/vegetables.

• Waštéwalake or Waštéwalake šni

Write the two words on the board. Then take a picture of one of your favorite fruits and say e.g.: **Zíškopela kiŋ wašté. Waštéwalake.** Repeat with another fruit/vegetable and then ask the children if they guessed what **waštéwalake** means {I like}. Encourage and help them with hints.

Then ask them to say **waštéwalake** or **waštéwalake šni** in response to various fruits and vegetables you name/show. The same activity can be done in pairs and groups.

• Zíškopela waštéyalaka hwo/he?

Ask the children to look at the characters on the previous page and to try to guess what they are saying. Encourage them and give hints.

Then write **waštéyalaka hwo/he?** {do you like?} on the board, and start asking the children questions like: **Thíŋpsiŋla waštéyalaka hwo/he?** {Do you like turnips?}. Ask several children individually, ask them to respond with **Háŋ, waštéwalake** or **Hiyá, waštéwalake šni**.

Then they can ask you. Children love asking their teachers questions about their likes and dislikes. Take advantage of it. Moreover, if you show that you like most of the fruits and vegetables, you can motivate good eating habits in your students as fruits and vegetables are very important in a healthy diet.

• Tell me

Tell me a fruit that begins with **tȟ** (**tȟaspáŋ**);
Tell me a vegetable beginning with **th** (**thíŋpsiŋla**).
Tell me a vegetable beginning with **k** (**kuŋkúŋ**) etc.

Notes: The illustration shows plums growing wildly in the plains area, not the commercially sold plums, which are darker purple. Two reviewers gave a variant for strawberries: **wazíškeča**.

wičhágnaška, čhuŋwíyapehe, tȟaspáŋzi, zíškopela, tȟaspáŋ, wažúšteča,
tȟaspáŋ pȟéstola, kȟáŋta, čhaŋpȟá, wagmúšpaŋšni

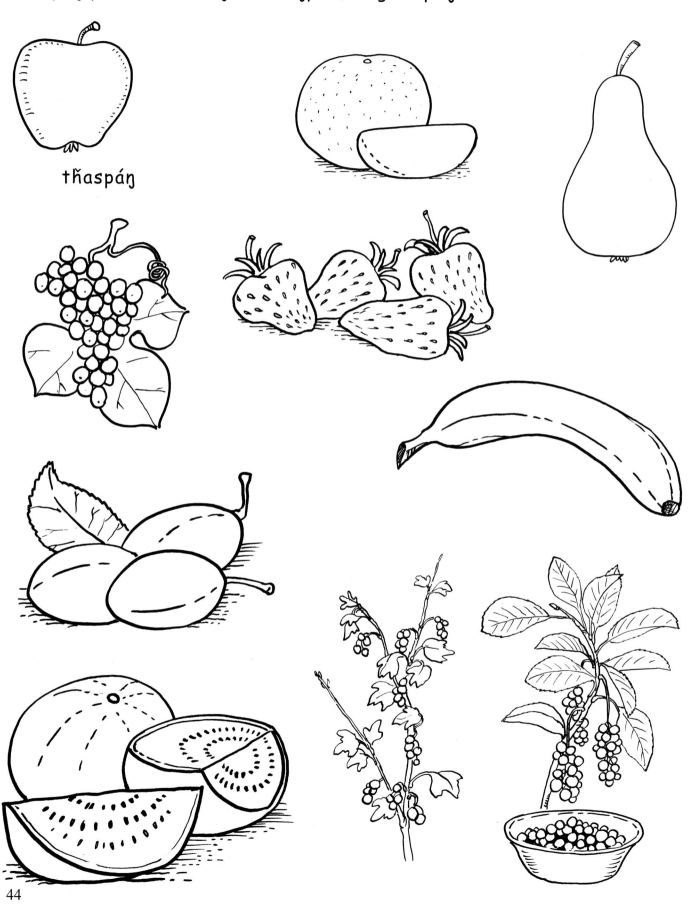

tȟaspáŋ

44

ȷžíŋžiŋtka bló pšíŋ thíŋpsiŋla waȟpé iŋkpážiži pȟaŋǧí zizí kuŋkúŋ

maȟpíya

maȟpíya   aŋpétu wí

obláye

otȟúŋwahe

pahá

blé

wakpála

wakpá

ȟaŋté

pȟeží

pȟežíȟota   uŋkčéla

aŋpétu wí, pahá, wakpá, ȟé, haŋhépi wí, maȟpíya, wičháȟpi, obláye,
čhúŋšoke, blé

čhóthi, wazí, wáǧačhaŋ, otȟúŋwahe, pȟežíȟota, waȟpé, makȟá, íŋyaŋ,

haŋkú, waȟčá, uŋkčéla, pȟeží

ulary on pg. 105; **Sounds:** ejective stops, (pg. 99).

se the flashcard exercises (page 90–93) to introduce new
lary.

fterwards, use the Lesson Page to reinforce the vocabulary.
e children to study the picture for a few minutes. Have the
n listen to the words spoken by you or from the audio CD.
this, and this time have the children repeat after you and
t the pictures. Give them instructions like: **Wáǧačhaŋ waŋ
azo wo!** {Show me a cottonwood.} Children point to the

proper thing in the picture. They can do the same activity in pairs.
Introduce: **Táku (čha) waŋláka hwo/he?** ➔ **Íŋyaŋ waŋ
waŋbláke.**

• Review **waštéwalake/waštéwalake šni.** The children can say
which things in the picture they like and dislike.

Note: Pahá is a generic word for "hill" or "hills." A lonely hill
like that in the picture is sometimes called **pažóla.** A variant of
waȟčá {flower} is **wanáȟča.**

49

tȟaló

wagmíza

aǧúyapi

waháŋpi

psíŋ

wígli-uŋ-káǧapi

omníča

hoǧáŋ

wítka

asáŋpi sutá

wóžapi

aǧúyapi skúyela

pápa

čhaŋháŋpi

Loyáčhiŋ he?

Háŋ, líla lowáčhiŋ.

Wóžapi líla waštéwalake.

mní   waȟpékȟalyapi   asáŋpi   tȟaspáŋ haŋpí   tȟaspáŋzi haŋpí

Líla ímapuza.

Mní yatkáŋ yo!

apȟópapi   wakȟályapi

For Teachers and Parents (Unit 12)

ocabulary on pg. 105. **Sounds:** clusters **bl, gm, gn, gl,** (instructions on pg. 99).

ach the food and drink vocabulary with the flashcard vities (page 90–93). Divide the vocabulary into two s. Afterwards, practice with these activities:

Put a food item flashcard on the board and write **wóyute** e it. Put a card with a drink item flashcard on the board write **wóyatke** above it. The students should repeat after **wóyute, wóyatke.** Call on individual students to se a flashcard and match it with a group.

fterwards, name individual foods and drinks. The nts should respond with **wóyute** or **wóyatke.** Repeat or w this in the next class, this time without the pictures. more advanced students use: **Kapȟópapi kiŋ wóyatke a. –** {Pop is a drink.}

Review of Waštélaka: The teacher names a food or item and calls on a child. The child responds with éwalake or waštéwalake šni according to his/her likes dislikes.

Ask individual students questions like: **Asáŋpi éyalaka hwo/he?** {Do you like milk?}. Students nd with: **Háŋ, waštéwalake,** or **Hiyá, waštéwalake** The students can do the same exercise in pairs.

owáchiŋ {I am hungry}, Ímapuza {I am thirsty}

d the dialogue on the food page and ask the children to nd guess what the characters are saying. The context d help the students to guess the correct answer. If not, them more hints.

en write on the board **lowáchiŋ** {I am hungry}. Ask the nts to repeat the word after you.

en write on the board **líla** {very}. Have the students t **Líla lowáchiŋ** after you or the audio CD.

Call upon individual children to tell you that they are very hungry. Each time give them a flashcard of a food, vegetable or fruit and say something like: **[Tȟaspáŋ] yúta yo/ye.** {Eat an [apple].}. After all or most of the children have received cards, ask them if they remember how to say "Eat!" Explain that men say **yúta yo** and women say **yúta ye** for "Eat!" Afterwards, say **Líla lowáchiŋ** addressing individual children and have them respond with: **[Aǧúyapi] yúta yo/ye,** and give you the card.

Older students can practice in pairs, using dialogues like:
A) **Loyáchiŋ hwo/he?** ➔ B) **Háŋ, lowáchiŋ.**
A) **Aǧúyapi yúta ye!** ➔ B) **Philámayaye.**

• Use the strategy and activities explained above for **ímapuza** {I am thirsty} (and **Ínipuza hwo/he?** {Are you thirsty}).

• Thirsty or Hungry?

Write the words **Loyáchiŋ** and **Ínipuza** on the board and practice their pronunciation. Then tell the children that you are going to name something you want to eat or drink. Have them tell you whether you are thirsty or hungry:

Teacher: **Hoǧáŋ wachíŋ.** ➔ Students: **Loyáchiŋ.**
Teacher: **Mní wachíŋ.** ➔ Students: **Ínipuza.**

Ask the students if they remember how to say "I want" (**wachíŋ**). Reverse roles. The children say what they want.

• Eating Habits

Ask about Bob and Gary on the following page in ways like this: **Bob tȟaspáŋ waštélaka hwo/he?** {Does Bob like apples?} ➔ **Hiyá, waštélake šni.**

(Use this activity to promote healthy eating habits.)

Note: A colloquial pronunciation of **wakȟályapi** is **wakȟálapi.**

52

Hokšíla kiŋ lé **B**ob ečíyapi.

Hokšíla kiŋ lé **G**ary ečíyapi.

Bob táku waštélaka he?

Gary táku waštélaka he?

Write "**B**" next to the things you think Bob likes.

Write "**G**" next to the things you think Gary likes.

53

píško

waŋblí

čhaŋšká

ikpísaŋla

tȟatȟáŋka

tȟáȟča

hečá

wábloša

tȟašíyagnuŋpa

šuŋgmánitu

kimímela

gnugnúšk

pispíza

pȟahíŋ

siŋtéȟla

maká

uŋkčépagmigma

maštíŋsk

Vocabulary on pg. 105; **Sounds:** glottal stop (pg. 100).

This lesson unit is devoted to common and [cu]lturally-relevant plains animals. Children enjoy learning [ab]out animals as well as animal names. This provides an [op]portunity to practice and review sentence structures, [ve]rbs, and modifiers that can be used with animal names. [In]troduce new vocabulary with the help of flashcard [ac]tivities (see pages 90–93). Make children aware of and [pr]actice the pronunciation difference between **hečá** {turkey [vul]ture} and **héčha** {to be such, to belong to a class (of [no]uns)}. After the children are familiar with the Lakota [wo]rds for animals, do the following activities:

Put the flashcard with a deer on the board and write [wa]mákȟaškaŋ above it. Then put the flashcard with one of [the] birds on another side of the board, and write **ziŋtkála** [ab]ove it. Do the same with one of the three insects and [wr]ite: **wablúška**. Then ask the children to repeat after you: [wa]mákȟaškaŋ, ziŋtkála, wablúška.

[T]hen show another flashcard and ask one of the children [to] add it to one of the three groups. Have a child come and [tak]e a flashcard from you and then add it to the appropriate [gro]up. Continue until all the flashcards are divided into [gro]ups.

[H]old on to the card with the rattlesnake and in the end put [it] on the board under a new category, **zuzéča**. In this [acti]vity the generic word **zuzéča** – {snake} is used as a [cate]gory. (According to some native speakers snakes belong [to t]he same group as insects.)

With the cards still on the board, ask the children to say [the] group of the animal you name, in ways like:

[T]eacher: **tȟatȟáŋka** ➔ Student: **wamákȟaškaŋ**

[T]eacher: **hečá** ➔ Student: **ziŋtkála**, etc.

Put the flashcards away and tell the children that you [are] going to find out if they can say **ziŋtkála**, [wa]mákȟaškaŋ, **wablúška**, **zuzéča** without seeing the [pict]ures. Then name individual animals, birds and insects.

[W]ith older students, have them say sentences like this: [Tȟa]tȟáŋka kiŋ wamákȟaškaŋ héčha. {A buffalo is an [anim]al.}

Put the deer flashcard on the board and write **tȟáŋka** [abov]e it. Then put the butterfly card on the board and write [čík'a]la above it. Ask the children to decide which of the [anim]als are **tȟáŋka** and which are **čík'ala**. Show one card [at a] time and call on the children to add them to one of the [two] groups. If you don't like a child's choice or if a child [can'] decide, ask the other children to help make the [deci]sion (by saying **tȟáŋka** or **čík'ala**). (Children usually [mak]e such decisions by comparing the size of an animal [to] themselves. In any case, you should make them feel [that] the decision is really up to them.)

[On]ce all the animals are divided between big and small, [ask t]he children to say **tȟáŋka** or **čík'ala** in response to you [nami]ng animals as in: **Teacher: maštíŋska ➔ Student: [čík'a]la).

[Y]ou can do similar activities with other characteristics

of animals, such as animals that walk (**máni**) versus those that fly (**kiŋyáŋ**), those that are loud (**hótȟaŋka** or **hotȟúŋ**), and those that make no noise (**iníla úŋ**).

• Review **waštéwalake** {I like} and **waštéwalake šni** {I don't like}. Show or name individual animals. The children respond with one of the verbs.

• With older or more advanced classes, introduce the infix -**wičha**- for plural animate objects. Try this activity:

Put a picture of a buffalo on the board. Write and say: **Tȟatȟáŋka waŋ waŋbláke.** {I see a buffalo.} Then, put another picture of a buffalo on the board. Write and say: **Tȟatȟáŋka núŋpa waŋwíčhablake.** {I see two buffalo.} Let the children practice with other animals. Have them write and say the sentences on their own. Afterwards, ask them: "When do we use -**wičha**-?" Children should respond with something like: "When we talk about more than one animal." Then, take a book (or put in on the table) and say: **Wówapi waŋ waŋbláke.** Add another book and say: **Wówapi núŋpa waŋbláke.** Then ask the children again: "Do you know when to use -**wičha**-?" Children: "Only when talking about animals (and people)."

• These same guidelines will be used for the vocabulary in units 23 and 24. After the students know the animal terms from all three lessons, repeat the above activities with all the animals. This could be done if you have some spare time at the end of the school year or if you want to have a playful class before the holidays.

• After finishing unit 15 you can use the animals in units 13, 23 and 24 to review animate plural, as in:

Teacher: Wablúška kiŋ tónapi hwo/he?

Student: (Wablúška kiŋ) yámnipi.

T: Ziŋtkála kiŋ tónapi hwo/he? ➔ **S: Ziŋtkála kiŋ šákpepi.**

T: Zuzéča kiŋ tónapi hwo/he? ➔ **S: Zuzéča kiŋ waŋžíla.**

Note 1: Some Lakota animal names are differentiated between male and female. The textbook pictures refer only to the male term. Some Lakota people use **tȟatȟáŋka** {buffalo bull} as a generic name for buffalo, others state it can only be used for "buffalo bull". Another term for buffalo bull is **pteblóka**, while buffalo cow is **ptewíŋyela**. **Pté** and **pteȟčáka** are other generic terms for buffalo (also used for a buffalo herd). **Note 2:** A more recent pronunciation of **šuŋgmánitu** is **šuŋgmáyetu**. Another less commonly used term for coyote is **mayášleča** or **yašlé**. **Note 3:** **Ikpísaŋla** {pronghorn} is also known as **niǧésaŋla**. **Note 4:** **Čhaŋšká** {red-tailed hawk}, the most common hawk on the northern plains, is also referred to as **čhaŋšká upíǧi** {red-tailed **čhaŋšká**}. Other kinds of hawks are called **čhetáŋ**. This term is widely used and tends to be the preferred word for hawks in general. **Note 5:** Some speakers use **Waŋblí** as a generic term for both types of eagles (golden eagle and bald eagle). Specific terms for eagles in Lakota are: **waŋblí** {adult golden eagle}, **waŋblí glešká** {young golden eagle}, **anúŋkȟasaŋ** {bald eagle}. The picture shows a young golden eagle. **Note 6:** Make the students aware of the pronunciation difference between **makȟá** {ground, earth, dirt} and **maká** {skunk}. **Note 7:** **Kimímila** is a variation of **kimímela**. **Note 8:** Both **maštíŋska** and **maštíŋčala** are used for jackrabbit.

55

1. Can you color the animals? Do you know their Lakota names?

píško   čhaŋšká   siŋtéȟla   tȟáȟča   gnugnúška

ikpísaŋla   waŋblí   maká   tȟatȟáŋka

56

2. Can you color the animals? Do you know their Lakota names?

maštíŋčala   kimímela   tȟašíyagnuŋpa   uŋkčépagmigma

pȟahíŋ   wábloša   pispíza   hečá   šuŋgmánitu

57

lečhála / tȟéča   tȟaŋníla

tȟéča   káŋ

pȟáŋžela   sutá

yuǧáŋ   natȟák<u>a</u>

čhép<u>a</u> tȟamáheča

óta   čónala

háŋsk<u>a</u>   ptéčela

tké   kap'óžela

ȟ'aŋhí   lúzahaŋ

čhatkáyatakiya išláyatakiya

šáp<u>a</u>   šápe šni

haŋtéšič**a** čhaŋtéwašte

hótȟaŋk**a**   iníla

waŋkáta

spáy**a**   púz**a**

ožúla   henála / waníč**a**

khúta

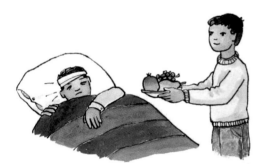

khúž**a**   zaŋní

šíč**a**   wašté

tȟokáhe

eháke

owáŋyaŋg šíč**a**   owáŋyaŋg wašté

kȟát**a**   sní

Use the flashcard activities (pg. 90-93). **Vocabulary** and instructions pg. 106; **Sounds**: 100.

khukhúše

šúŋkawakȟáŋ

šúŋka

igmú

ptegléška

iktómi

waglékšuŋ

wakíŋyela

kȟokȟóyaȟ'aŋla

maǧá

maǧáksiča

itȟúŋkala

Vocabulary on pg. 106.
Sounds: consonant clusters, on pg. 100.

Animate plural

The main object of this unit is to understand how the animate plural ending –pi is used (with people and animals). There is less vocabulary in this unit in order to give more time to demonstrate and practice this concept. At the K-1 level, students only need a passive knowledge of the grammatical rules in this lesson. With older or more advanced classes you may want to encourage work towards active usage.

- Introduce new vocabulary through flashcard games (cf. pages 90–93).
- After the children are familiar with the new words, ask them to open their textbooks and work with the Lesson Page like this:

Lená …. héčhapi.

- Point at the dog and say:
Teacher: Lé táku hwo/he? Student: Lé šúŋka héčha.
Repeat with cat and spider.
- Point at a group of animals in the picture and say:
Lená táku héčhapi hwo/he? {What are these?}
Answer yourself if the children can't do so:
Lená khukhúše héčhapi. {These are pigs.}
If necessary repeat with other animals.
The children should be able to grasp the usage and meaning of Lená … héčhapi as opposed to Lé … héčha.
Ask the children to point at a group of animals and ask you in this way: Lená táku héčhapi hwo/he? Repeat until all the children have spoken.
Then reverse roles. You ask them and they answer (with plural in Lená and héčhapi).

Write on the board a few example sentences, e.g.:
Lená maǧá héčhapi.
Lená ptegléška héčhapi.

Then ask the children: "Why do you think we have –pi here?"
They should be able to formulate an answer. If not, help them (e.g. "It is there because there are many animals".)

To ensure that the children understand the difference between animate and inanimate plural, try this: Hold up two pens or touch two chairs and say: Lená wíčazo héčha.; Lená oákaŋke héčha.
Then point at two boys and say: Lená hokšíla héčhapi.
Do this at the end of class or follow it by a new activity.

Lená tónapi hwo/he?

After reviewing the Lená … héčhapi sentence, start introducing the suffix –pi with numbers.
Ask the children to count the animals in the picture.

Then tell them that you will say the number of animals in a group and they will point at and name the animal group. Try it like this:
Teacher: núŋpapi ➔ Student: waglékšuŋ
Teacher: záptaŋpi ➔ Student: khukhúše
Teacher: tópapi ➔ Student: šúŋkawakȟáŋ
Teacher: waŋžíla ➔ Student: iktómi / šúŋka / igmú
Ask them: "Children, did you notice what I added to the numbers?" They should respond with something like: "You added –pi, because there are several animals"

Reverse the activity. The teacher names the animals and children say numbers in plural. With more advanced classes you may practice this in full sentences:
Lená tónapi hwo/he? ➔ Lená núŋpapi.
Ptegléška kiŋ tónapi hwo/he? ➔ Ptegléška kiŋ yámnipi.
Afterwards, let them name a group of animals and you tell them the number of animals as in:
Children: khukhúše ➔ Teacher: záptaŋpi etc.

Colors in Animate Plural

Ask the children to point to the group of animals who have the color you name as in:
Teacher: ȟolȟótapi ➔ Student: wakíŋyela
Teacher: šašápi ➔ Student: kȟokȟéyaȟ'aŋla
Teacher: skaskápi ➔ Student: maǧá
Teacher: šastáŋpi ➔ Student: khukhúše
Teacher: zizípi ➔ Student: šúŋkawakȟáŋ

Note: With the exception of compounded colors terms (e.g. tȟózi), colors are both reduplicated and pluralized when referring to animals. Some speakers don't reduplicate colors in animate plural, but many do. The reduplication may be referring to the numerous hairs or feathers of animals.
Practice sentences like this: Maǧá kiŋ (lená) skaskápi.

Review of Sizes

Teacher: Ptegléška kiŋ tȟáŋka naíŋš čík'ala he?
Student: Ptegléška kiŋ tȟáŋka.

Note 1: There are many synonyms and local variants for "chicken (hen)". These include: kȟokȟóyaȟ'aŋla, kȟokȟéyaȟ'aŋla, kȟokȟáyaȟ'aŋla, but there may be others. Use whatever variant is common in your area.
Note 2: The word khukhúše {pig} sometimes appears as khukhúša. **Note 3:** Šúŋkawakȟáŋ {horse} is colloquially pronounced "šúŋkakȟaŋ". Children should begin with the careful or "yat'íŋsya" or slow pronunciation. The word tȟašúŋka is only used to express "his/her horse" and will be introduced later.
Note 4: Ptegléška {cow} is often pronounced ptebléška. **Note 5:** Some speakers reduplicate the animate plural of colors, others do not, as in: Ziŋtkála kiŋ šašápi. versus Ziŋtkála kiŋ šápi.

1. Lé táku hwo/he?

Lé **šúŋkawakȟáŋ** héčha.

Lé **šúŋka** héčha.

Lé **itȟúŋkala** héčha.

Lé **khukhúše** héčha.

Lé **wakíŋyela** héčha.

Lé **kȟokȟóyaȟʼaŋla** héčha.

Lé **ptegléška** héčha.

Lé **maǧáksiča** héčha.

Lé **maǧá** héčha.

Lé **igmú** héčha.

Lé **iktómi** héčha.

Lé **waglékšuŋ** héčha.

2. Lená tónapi hwo/he?

How many are there?

Lená **šakówiŋpi**.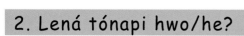

Lená _____.

Lená _____.

Lená _____.

Lená _____.

Lená _____.

Ask and answer: Lená tákupi he?   Lená maǧáksiča héčhapi.

62

Lená **šašápi** _____ .

Khukhúše kiŋ lená

_____ .

Lená _____ .

Šúŋka kiŋ lená

_____ .

Lená _____ .

Kȟokȟéyaȟ'aŋla kiŋ

lená _____ **šašápi** _____ .

Lená _____ .

Maǧáksiča kiŋ lená

_____ .

Lená _____ .

Lená _____ .

Itȟúŋkala kiŋ lená

_____ .

Lená šúŋkawakȟáŋ héčhapi.

Šúŋkawakȟáŋ hú tópa yukȟáŋpi.   Waglékšuŋ hú núŋpa yukȟáŋpi.

Šúŋka núŋpa ǧiǧípi. Wakíŋyela tópa ȟolȟótapi. Maǧá yámni skaskápi.
     Šúŋkawakȟáŋ yámni sapsápapi.   Igmú núŋpa saŋsáŋpi.

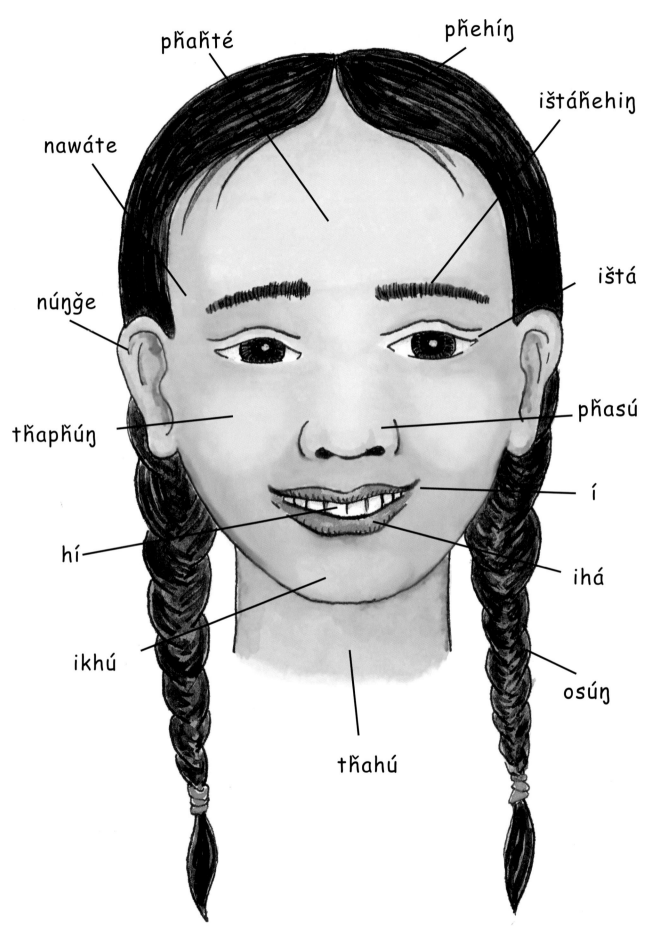

pȟahté

pȟehíŋ

ištáȟehiŋ

nawáte

ištá

núŋǧe

pȟasú

tȟapȟúŋ

í

hí

ihá

ikhú

osúŋ

tȟahú

Vocabulary on pg. 106. **Sounds** on pg. 100.

In this unit the vocabulary is introduced and practiced through activities involving children's own faces. If teachers want extra materials, they can make their own handout activities, such as having the children match words with a picture of a face.

There are 14 facial or head parts in this unit. Introduce them to the children in two groups:

1) **í, núŋǧe, pȟasú, ištá, pȟehíŋ, hí, pȟaȟté**
2) **ihá, ikhú, tȟahú, tȟapȟúŋ, nawáte, ištáȟehiŋ, osúŋ, ité**

Teachers should have the students be very familiar with the first group of terms, before they teach the second group.

•Touch your nose with your index finger and say **pȟasú**. Ask the children to do the same and repeat the word after you. Repeat with other words from the first group. Alternatively, use the audio CD. Demonstrate by touching when you hear the word.

After you feel that the children are quite familiar with the words, reinforce them through the following activities:

•Ask the children to touch the facial part you name. Then say: **Pȟasú églutȟaŋ po/pe!** {Touch your nose!}. **Núŋǧe églutȟaŋ po/pe!** {Touch your ears!} etc.

• Later, ask the children to name the facial part that you touch.

Do the same sequence of activities for the second group of facial parts.

Play the game Simon Heyé:
Children touch the named facial/body part only if **Simon heyé** {Simon says} is said first. For instance:
Simon heyé: Natá églutȟaŋ po! [Children touch.]
Simon heyé: Sí églutȟaŋ po! [Children touch.]
Ikhú églutȟaŋ po! [Children do not touch.]

With the more advanced classes, teach these sentence structures:
Pȟehíŋ masápsape. {My hair is black.}
Ištá maǧíǧi. {My eyes are brown.}
And also:
Ištá núŋpa mayúkȟe. {I have two eyes.}
Núŋǧe núŋpa mayúkȟe. {I have two ears.}
Pȟasú waŋžíla mayúkȟe. {I have one nose.}
With advanced classes, add the word **čheží** {tongue}.

How many?
Ask the children to give the number of the facial parts you name, as in:

í => **waŋží**, **pȟasú** => **waŋží**, **núŋǧe** => **núŋpa**, **tȟahú** => **waŋží**, **nawáte** => **núŋpa**, **ištá** => **núŋpa**, **pȟehíŋ** = **óta**, **hí** => **óta**, etc. Introduce **óta** beforehand.

Older or more advanced students can create sentences of this type: **Í waŋžíla mayúkȟe.** {I have only one mouth.} **Ištá núŋpa mayúkȟe.** {I have two eyes.} **Iktómi sí šaglóǧaŋ yukȟé.** {The spider has eight legs.} etc.

Play with Rhymes
Children love rhymes and songs. They are enjoyable and help with word memorization and sentence structures.

Most of the facial parts have at least one rhyming companion. Try playing a game with the children like this:

Tell them that you will say a facial part. They must respond with one that rhymes and at the same time touch the facial part they name, such as: **hí – í.**

Here are the pairs: **ikhú ⟷ pȟasú ⟷ tȟahú; i ⟷ hí; osúŋ ⟷ tȟapȟúŋ; pȟehíŋ ⟷ ištáȟehiŋ; ihá ⟷ ištá; pȟaȟté ⟷ nawáte ⟷ ité ⟷ núŋǧe**

Play "Who is it?"
Tell the children that you are going to think of someone in the class and they must guess who it is. They should ask questions such as: **Pȟehíŋ háŋska yukȟáŋ hwo/he?** {Does he/she have long hair?}, **Uŋzóǧe sápa úŋ hwo/he?** {Is he/she wearing black pants?} etc.

With advanced students, demonstrate and explain possessive pronouns. For the 1st person singular, the prefix **ma-** or **mi-** is used (**miíte** {my face}, **mapȟéhiŋ** {my hair}. For the 2nd person singular, the prefix **ni-** is used, e.g. **nipȟéhiŋ** {your hair}.

With older students, make sure to explain that **mitȟáwa/nitȟáwa/tȟáwa** are not used with body parts.

Independent personal pronouns (like **mitȟáwa**) are not used with body parts (and kinship terms). This is one of the most common errors students make when translating from English to Lakota.

Note 1: **Pȟóǧe** is given by some speakers as the term for "nose", though most suggest this refers to "nostrils". Another, more specific, term for "nostrils" is **pȟóǧeoȟloka**.
Note 2: **Natá** is only used for human heads. The heads of animals and things are called **pȟá**.
Note 3: **Núŋǧe** is only used for human ears. **Nakpá** is used for animal ears.

nážiŋ   íyotak**a**   yaŋk**á**   yuŋk**á**

wayáwa   wówa   wówa itówapi ow

wót**a**   wayátk**aŋ**

iyúŋk**a**   ištíŋm**a**   iháŋbl**a**   kiktá

iglúžaža   hi-kpážaža   glastó

kipázo   waŋyáŋk**a**

kaȟ'ól iyéy**a**   yukȟáp**a**

wóglak**a**   anáǧoptaŋ

hakíč'uŋ   glušlók

For **vocabulary** and **instructions** see pg. 106.

pȟóskil yúz**a**   kigná   ipútȟak**a**

máni   íŋyaŋk**a**

k'ú   ičú

nuŋw**áŋ**

páŋ / kipáŋ   ožíži

k'íŋ   égnak**a**

šuŋkákaŋyaŋk**a**   čhéy**a**   iȟá   škát**a**

67

Wimáčhaȟčala. Lél maŋké.

Iníla yaŋká ye! Tȟakóža kiŋ ištíŋme kštó.

Lakȟóta homákšila.

Waímnaŋke.

wičháȟčala   winúȟčala

wičhíŋčala

hokšíla

Lakȟóta wiŋmáyaŋ.

Igmú sápa waŋ bluhá.

Lakȟóta wimáčhaša.

Tȟaspáŋ waŋ wáte.

Wamášiču. Ímapuza čha mni-blátke.

wíŋyaŋ

wičháša

wašíču

Čhaŋksáyuha hemáčha. Mawáni.

Waúŋspekhiya hemáčha. Waŋná nawážiŋ.

Wašíču wakȟáŋ hemáčha. Waŋná wabláwa.

čhaŋksáyuha

waúŋspekhiya

wašíču wakȟáŋ

68

cabulary on pg. 107. **Sounds** on pg. 100.

is unit introduces 10 terms, which describe people or cupations. Students will already be familiar with **hokšíla** oy} and **wičhíŋčala** {girl}.

me of the activities for this unit are complex and the cher should adjust them according to the students' age.

Review the following dialogue

túwe hwo/he? {Who are you?}
bert Jumping Eagle hé miyé. {I am Robert Jumping gle.}
na Running Elk miyé. {I am Dana Running Elk.}

Demonstrate and practice the following dialogue

táku hwo/he? {What are *you*?}
mákšila. or Hokšíla hemáčha. {I am a boy.}
máčhiŋčala. or Wičhíŋčala hemáčha. {I am a girl.}

u can extend the sentence like this:
kȟóta homákšila. / Lakȟóta hokšíla hemáčha.
m a Lakota boy.}
kȟóta wimáčhiŋčala. / Lakȟóta wičhíŋčala hemáčha.
m a Lakota girl.}

th older students, you can ask them to find out and define difference between **Nitúwe hwo/he?** {Who are you?} erring to your name) – and **Nitáku hwo/he?** {What are ?} (referring to your other types of identity, like tribe, upation etc.)

Use the flashcard activities (page 90–93) to introduce vocabulary.

may explain how the words portray the stages in life:
šíla {boy}, **wičháša** {man}, **wičháȟčala** {old man}
híŋčala {girl}, **wíŋyaŋ** {woman}, **winúȟčala** {old nan}.
th older students, add **kȟoškálaka** {young man} and ȟóškalaka {young woman} for the third stage of life. s will complete the explanation of the four stages itionally recognized in Lakota culture.

rk with the Lesson Page

Review of Yuhá (I.):

háša kiŋ lé táku (čha) yuhá hwo/he? {What does the have?} ➔ Tȟaspáŋ (waŋ yuhá). {(He has an) apple.}
šíču kiŋ lé táku (čha) yuhá hwo/he? {What does the te man have?} ➔ Wíyatke (waŋ yuhá). {(He has a) glass.}
yaŋ kiŋ lé táku (čha) yuhá hwo/he? {What does the an have?} ➔ Igmú sápa (waŋ yuhá). {(She has a)

ŋspekhiya kiŋ lé táku (čha) yuhá hwo/he? {What the teacher have?} ➔ Wówapi (waŋ yuhá). {(She has ok.}

Review of Yuhá (II.) (Who Questions)

á tȟaspáŋ waŋ yuhá? {Who has an apple?} – háša kiŋ. {The man.} etc.

Review of Yuhá (III.) ("Yes" and "No" Questions)

Waúŋspekhiya kiŋ lé igmú waŋ yuhá hwo/he? {Does the teacher have a cat?} ➔ **Háŋ / Hiyá.**

Review the Verb Úŋ (to Wear)

Tuwá ógle sápa waŋ úŋ hwo/he? {Who is wearing a black shirt?} ➔ **Čhaŋksáyuha kiŋ.** {The policeman.}
Tuwá ógle zigzíča tȟózi waŋ úŋ? {Who is wearing a green sweater?} ➔ **Winúȟčala kiŋ.** {The old woman.}

Other Verbs

With older students, you can review some other verbs, such as, **Tuwá nážiŋ hwo/he?** {Who is standing?}; **Tuwá máni hwo/he?** {Who is walking?}; **Tuwá wayátkaŋ hwo/he?** {Who is drinking?} and **Tuwá wóglaka hwo/he?** {Who is talking?} etc.

"I" – forms

Introduce "I"-forms with **hemáčha** (e.g.: **Wičháša hemáčha** {I am a man.}). Practice them like this. Explain to the students that you will say a verb, and they should react with the appropriate person and "I"-form, as in:
Teacher: Igmú waŋ luhá. ➔ **Student: Wíŋyaŋ hemáčha.**
T: Ógle sápa waŋ núŋ. ➔ **S: Čhaŋksáyuha hemáčha.**
T: Ništíŋme. ➔ **S: Wičhíŋčala hemáčha.**
T: Wóyaglake. ➔ **S: Winúȟčala hemáčha.**

You may explain and demonstrate the alternate "I"-form of nouns that refer to life stages:
homákšila {I am a boy}
wimáčhaša {I am a man}
kȟomáškalaka {I am a young man}
wimáčhaȟčala {I am an old man}
wimáčhiŋčala {I am a girl}
wiŋmáyaŋ {I am a woman}
wimákȟoškalaka {I am a young woman}
wimánuȟčala {I am an old woman}

Who has what?

Provide the children with various flashcards of people, animals and things. The students should choose one card with a person and another with a thing or animal. When called on, they should hold them up and say sentences like:
Wičháša kiŋ lé šúŋka (sápa) waŋ yuhá. {This man has a (black) dog.}
Hokšíla kiŋ lé tȟápa waŋ yuhá. {This boy has a ball.}
Later, they can identify themselves with the character on their flashcard and say similar sentences in the first person singular: **Hokšíla hemáčha. Tȟápa waŋ bluhá.** {I am a boy. I have a ball.}

Note: Variations for policeman are: **čhaŋksáyuha** in Pine Ridge, **wawóyuspa** in Cheyenne River and **akíčhita** in Rosebud.

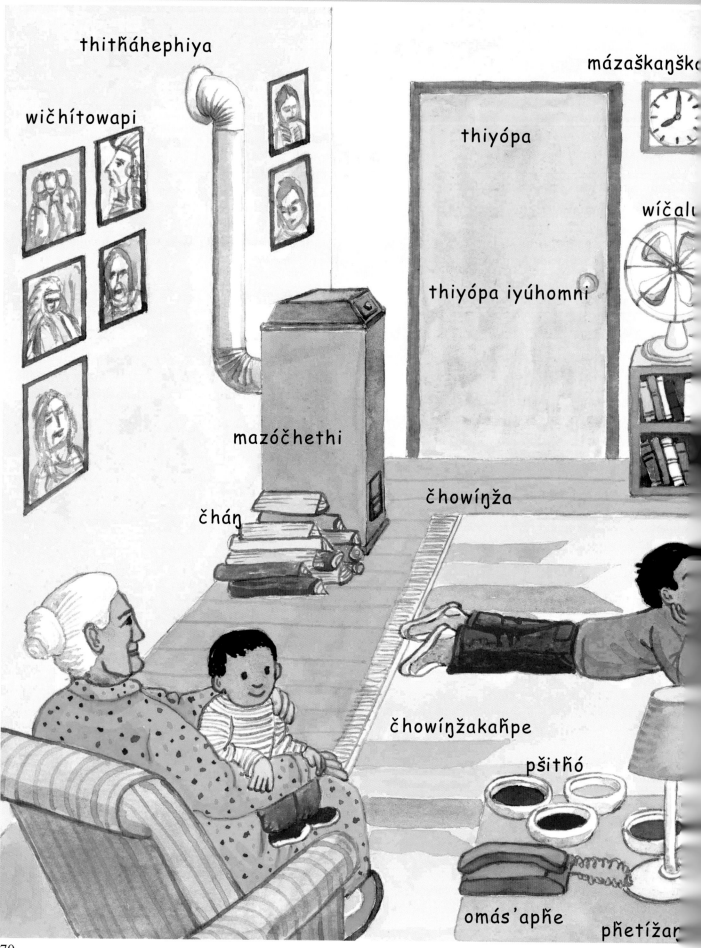

thitȟáhephiya

wičhítowapi

mázaškaŋškc

thiyópa

wíčalı

thiyópa iyúhomni

mazóčhethi

čhowíŋža

čháŋ

čhowíŋžakaȟpe

pšitȟó

omás'apȟe

pȟetížaŋ

Vocabulary on pg. 107. **Sounds** on pg. 100.
Use flashcard activities to teach the vocabulary of the living room items (page 90–93).
Review the verbal form **waŋbláke** {I see}.

- ### Reviewing Colors (I.)
Using the new vocabulary terms, you can review colors, in ways like:

Čhowíŋža kiŋ ǧí. {The floor is brown.}

Oákaŋke kiŋ tȟózi na šá. {The chair is green and red.}

Ikȟáŋčhola kiŋ tȟó. {The radio is blue.}

Čhowíŋžakaȟpe kiŋ sáŋ na zí na ȟóta na šá. {The carpet is whitish, yellow, gray, and red.}

Wičhítenaškaŋškaŋ kiŋ sápe. {The television is black.}

Thiyópa kiŋ tȟózi. {The door is green.}

Mazóčhethi kiŋ šá. {The stove is red.}

Omás'apȟe kiŋ ȟóta/sápe. {The telephone is gray/black.}

Pšitȟó kiŋ šašá na tȟotȟó na zizí na skaská na sapsápe. {The beads are red, blue, yellow, white, and black.} etc.

- ### Reviewing Colors (II.) and Mitȟáwa
Have the children color the images on the following page. After they are done, they can describe their items using sentences like:

Thiyópa mitȟáwa kiŋ zí. {My door is yellow.}

Pȟetížaŋžaŋ mitȟáwa kiŋ tȟó. {My lamp is blue.} etc.

- ### Work in Pairs
Working in pairs, the students can ask each other about their pictures in ways like: **Omás'apȟe nitȟáwa kiŋ oówa tókča he?** {What color is your telephone?} ➔ **Hé šá.** {It is red.} Older students can talk about the things they have at their homes.

- ### Review of Bluhá/Luhá
Working in pairs, the students can ask each other about their pictures (or things at home) in ways like:

Omás'apȟe waŋží luhá he? {Do you have a telephone?}

Háŋ, omás'apȟe tȟó waŋ bluhá. {Yes, I have a blue telephone.}

- ### Review of Kinship Terms:
Tell the students something like this: "Imagine you are the girl in the picture. How would you address the people in the living room?"

Iná, até, thibló, misúŋ, kaká/tȟuŋkášila, uŋčí.

Afterwards, say: "Imagine you are the boy in the picture. How would you address the people in the living room?"

Iná, até, tȟaŋké, misúŋ, kaká/tȟuŋkášila, uŋčí.

- ### Review Clothing and Colors
Tell the students something like this: "Imagine you are either the girl or the boy. Tell us what everybody else in the living room is wearing."

Iná-waye kiŋ ógle šá úŋ.

Tȟuŋkášila-waye kiŋ uŋzóǧe tȟo na ógle šá úŋ.

Até-waye kiŋ ógle ská úŋ.

Uŋčí-waye kiŋ čhuwígnaka tȟózi úŋ.

Miyé ógle zí múŋ. etc.

The teacher can stimulate answers by asking questions like:

Tȟuŋkášila-yaye kiŋ táku (čha) úŋ hwo/he? {What is your grandfather wearing?}

Ógle šá úŋ. {He is wearing a red shirt.}
or:

Tuwá ógle ská úŋ? {Who is wearing a white shirt?}

Até-waye kiŋ. {My father.}

- ### Táku Tókȟuŋpi (Review of Verbs)
Ask the students what the individual people in the picture are doing, using constructions like:

Wičháȟčala kiŋ lé táku tókȟuŋ he? {What is the old man doing?} ➔ **(Hé) wóglake.** {He is talking.}

(In this case, a verb is used that the students are familiar with. Other verbs, such as **ohúŋkakaŋ** {he is storytelling} might be more appropriate. You may introduce this afterwards.)

Wičháša kiŋ lé táku tókȟuŋ he? {What is the man doing?} ➔ **(Hé) anáǧoptaŋ.** {He is listening.}

Hokšíla na wičhíŋčala kiŋ lená táku tókȟuŋpi he? {What are the boy and the girl doing?} ➔ **(Lená/Hená) anáǧoptaŋpi.** {They are listening.}

You can also introduce **wakšú** {to do beadwork} as in: **Wíŋyaŋ kiŋ lé wakšú.** {The woman is doing beadwork.}

- ### Homework
Ask the children to name things at home and then to ask their parents/grandparents about their colors in Lakota.

Note: A variant for "radio" is **ikȟáŋčhola kaȟwógyapi.**

73

ikčé wačhí wičháša

pȟežímignaka

oštéšteya wačhí

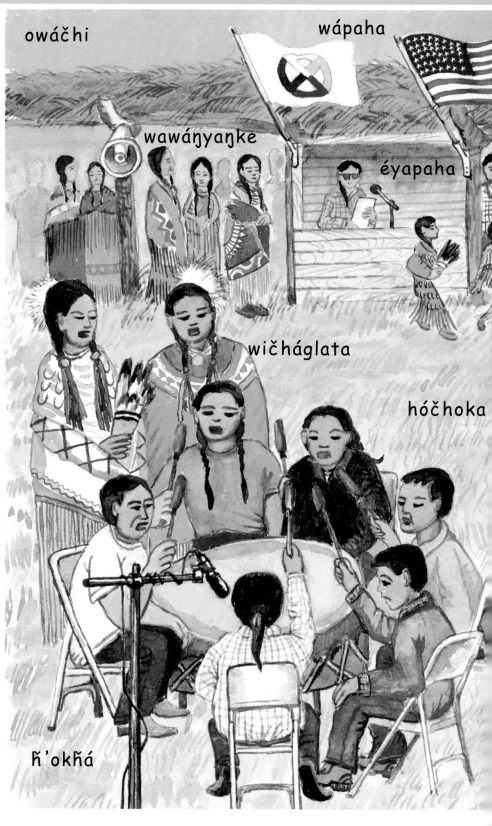

owáčhi

wápaha

wawáŋyaŋke

éyapaha

wičháglata

hóčhoka

ȟʼokȟá

čháŋčheǧa

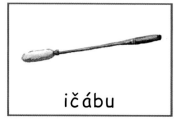

ičábu

waháčhaŋ

waȟpé wókheya

thiíkčeya

pazo Thimá Hiyúpi

ikčé wačhí wíŋyaŋ

šiná úŋ wačhí

snasná wačhí

íčalu

uŋkčéla káǧapi

pȟéša

Vocabulary on pg. 107; **Sounds**: more clusters, pg. 100.

This unit is designed as a review lesson and will enable you to review and reinforce much of the previously introduced vocabulary, such as verb forms and sentence structures.

To begin, stimulate the children with questions about their interests in pow-wows. Ask them whether they or their family members dance or sing. What are their favorite dances or songs?

Working with the Lesson Page
- **Review and Reinforce Verbs and Sentences**

T: **Táku (čha) waŋláka hwo/he?** {What do you see?}
S: **Pȟéša waŋ waŋbláke.** {I see a head roach.}
T: **Snasná wačhí waštéyalaka hwo/he?** {Do you like the jingle dress dance?}
S: **Háŋ, waštéwalake.** {Yes, I like it.}

- **Review the Traditional Clothing Items**

These are: **šiná** {blanket}; **haŋpíkčeka** {moccasins}; **huŋská** {leggings}; **wanápʼiŋ** {necklace}; **ógle** {shirt}; **tȟahá ógle** {leather shirt}; **čhuwígnaka** {dress}; **tȟahá čhuwígnaka** {leather dress}; and **čhegnáke** {breech cloth}. (You can add more specific vocabulary, such as **háŋpakšupi** {beaded moccasins} if you feel the need.)

You may want to review the traditional clothing presented in the Unit 7 Lesson Page.

- **Pow-wow Items**

These are: **pȟéša** {head roach}; **íčalu** {feather fan}; **waháčhaŋka** {shield}; and **uŋkčéla káǧapi** {bustle}.

The children should already know the word **uŋkčéla** {cactus} introduced in Unit 11. You may want to explain that **uŋkčéla káǧapi** means something like, "made in the shape of a cactus (with feathers pointing out like cactus spines)."

- **Review the Verb Yuhá**

Ask the children something like: "Can you tell me in Lakota what traditional clothes you have." You may give them an example by saying what you have, as in:
Haŋpíkčeka bluhá.
Íčalu waŋ bluhá. *
Huŋská bluhá. etc.
* Please, note that **waŋ** is used only with non-pair items.

- **Review colors, sizes, possessives**

Use the traditional clothing items to review modifiers (colors, sizes, possessives), in ways like this:

Colors (and Possessives)
Haŋpíkčeka mitȟáwa kiŋ tȟó na šá. {My moccasins are blue and red.}
Čhuwígnaka mitȟáwa kiŋ zí. {My dress is yellow.} etc.

Sizes (and Possessives)
Waháčhaŋka mitȟáwa kiŋ číkʼala. {My shield is small.}
Íčalu mitȟáwa kiŋ tȟáŋka. {My fan is big.}
Uŋkčéla káǧapi mitȟáwa kiŋ číkʼala. {My bustle is small.} etc.

- **Review the Kinship Terms**

Ask the children something like this: "What do your relatives do at a pow-wow? Do they dance? Do they sing? Do they like to watch the dancers?" (The term for "spectators" is **wawáŋyaŋke.**) Have the children respond using sentences like:

Iná-waye kiŋ šiná úŋ wačhí. {My mother is a shawl dancer.}
Até-waye kiŋ ȟʼokȟá wičháša héčha. {My father is a singer.}
Thibló-waye kiŋ oštéšteya wačhí. {My older brother is a fancy dancer. (a girl speaking)}
Čhiyé-waye kiŋ ikčé wačhí wičháša. {My older brother is a traditional dancer. (a boy speaking)} etc.

- **Review Vocabulary for People and Verbs**

While pointing at images on the Lesson Page, demonstrate sentences that describe what the people are doing. Afterwards, have the children say similar sentences.
Hokšíla kiŋ lé wačhí. {This boy is dancing.}
Wičhíŋčala kiŋ lé wačhí. {This girl is dancing.}
Wičháša kiŋ lé wawáŋyaŋke. {This man is watching.}
Wíŋyaŋ kiŋ lé lowáŋ. {This woman is singing.}

- **Uŋspé (To Know How)**

With older or more advanced students, introduce the following constructions:
Wačhí uŋmáspe. {I know how to dance. (I can dance).}
Lowáŋ uŋmáspe. {I know how to sing. (I can sing).}

Notes:
There are many variants for the pow-wow terms, particularly among the dance categories. Variants to those on the Lesson Page include: "Traditional Dance" – **Eháŋkʼehaŋ Wačhí**; "Women's Traditional Dance" – **Tȟahá Čhuwígnaka Ú**; "Shawl Dance" – **Sitóhomni Wačhí**; "Men's Fancy Dance" – **Sitóhomni Wačhí**; "Grass Dance" – **Kalála Wačhí** **Nitégleglèǧa Wačhí** / **Uŋzégleǧa Wačhí** / **Pȟežímignaka** **Pȟeží Wačhí**. Reviewers also suggested the term **Omá** **Wačhí**, but disagreed on which dance it referred to. A variant **Snasná Wačhí** is **Kasná Wačhí**. **Wapȟéša** is a variant of **pȟé** Most of the reviewers gave **okȟá** as the contemporary form **ȟʼokȟá** (or **ȟʼokȟá wičháša** {singers}). An additional varian "singer" is **lowáŋ wičháša**.

kiŋyékhiyapi

ȟemáni

thípi

GAS STATION

wigli oínažiŋ

pȟéta oínažiŋ
FIRE STATION

owáčhekiye

wóyute mas'óphiye

GROCERY STORE

mázaska th

owóte thípi

RESTAUR

oyúžužu thípi

mas'óphiye

TRADING POST

POST OFFICE

oíčhimani thípi

ARTS & CRAFTS

HOTEL

čhaŋksáyuha

okhúže thípi

wičhítenaškaŋškaŋ othí

wečhiŋkyaŋke áphiye

oyáte itȟókšu

iwátȟokšu

očháŋku

wáta

owáyawa

owáyawa itȟókšu

wówapi othí

GAS STATION

FIRE STATION

GROCERY STORE

RESTAUR

TRADING POST

POST OFFICE

ARTS & CRAFTS

HOTEL

Vocabulary on pg. 107.

22. Tȟatúye Tópa

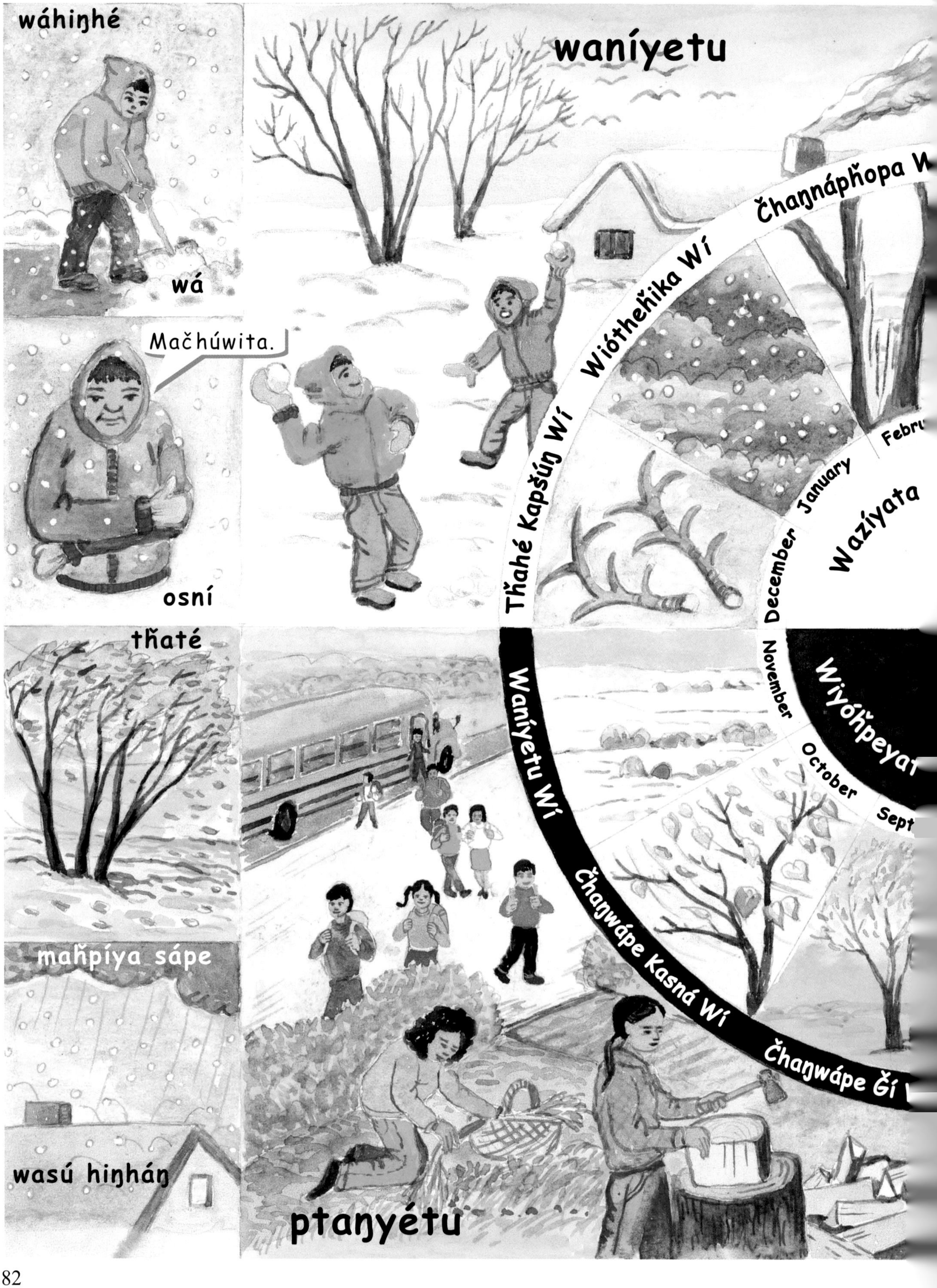
wáhiŋhé
wá
Mačhúwita.
osní
tȟaté
maȟpíya sápe
wasú hiŋháŋ
waníyetu
Čhaŋnápȟopa W
Wiótheȟika Wí
Tȟahé Kapšúŋ Wí
Febru
January
December
Waziyata
November
October
Sept
Wiyóȟpeya
Waníyetu Wí
Čhaŋwápe Kasná Wí
Čhaŋwápe Ǧí W
ptaŋyétu

wétu

mağážu

wígmuŋke

p'ó

omášte

Omákȟate.

okȟáta

wakíŋyaŋ hotȟúŋpi

wakíŋyaŋ tuŋwáŋpi

blokétu

táwičhayazaŋ Wí

Pȟeží Tȟó Wí

Čhaŋwápe Tȟó Wí

Thíŋpsiŋla Itkáȟča Wí

Čhaŋpȟá Sápa Wí

Wasútȟuŋ Wí

iyóhiyaŋpata

Itókağata

March

April

May

June

July

ust

Vocabulary on pg. 108. **Sounds** on pg. 100.

The colors that symbolize the four directions and seasons differ between communities and individuals. The Lesson Page shows the colors used in some communities on the Pine Ridge and the Cheyenne River reservations. Another very wide-spread variant of the four colors is: West = black, North = red, East = yellow, and South = white. Please have your students become familiar with whatever colors are common in your local community. Ideally, draw the four-direction circle, color it with the colors of your community and put it on a wall in the classroom to help the students become familiar with it. If the children see that the teacher respects cultural variations, it will teach them to honor and value diversity and richness in Lakota culture. Traditionally, the four-directions circle is oriented with the winter quarter up. You may want to make that clear to your students.

Lakota names of the months vary among communities. Also, most months have more than one name. The reviewers agreed that those chosen here belong among the most commonly used.

Most Lakota speakers today use English names for months when indicating the occurrence of events. Pre-reservation Lakota people used a lunar calendar with 13 lunar months. This calendar is incompatible with the 12-month western calendar. Today, the Lakota month names are used mostly in a ceremonial or formal context. The goal of this unit is not to teach active usage of the month names, but to have the students become aware of them and their meanings. Active usage will be introduced at higher levels.

The following activities should be adjusted to the students' age and to their reading ability.

- **What do the months mean?**

Teachers can explain that in traditional times, months were named after things that occurred in nature. Using the Lesson Page, have the students listen to the teacher or audio CD naming the months. Have them guess what the names mean. The students should already be familiar with many of the words used in month names, such as: **pȟeží, čhaŋpȟá, thíŋpsiŋla, tȟó, sápa, ǧí,** etc. Therefore, they should be able to guess many of the month names.

Explain that when referring to the color of leaves and grasses, **tȟó** {blue} is used to mean "green." Ask them to find the month names that include **tȟó** and to guess what the names mean, as in:

Pȟeží Tȟó Wí {April} = "The moon of green grass"
Ask the students: "Why do you think this month is called that?" (Answer: Because this moon occurs when the first green grass appears).

Čhaŋwápe Tȟó Wí {May} = "The moon of green leaves"
Ask the students: "Can you guess what **čhaŋwápe** means?" (Answer: "tree leaf/leaves".)

Ask: "How many months have a tree in their picture?" (Answer: "Four.") Read these month names with the children and write them in a column on the board:

Čhaŋwápe Tȟó Wí {May}
Čhaŋwápe Ǧí Wí {September}
Čhaŋwápe Kasná Wí {October}
Čhaŋnápȟopa Wí {February}

Ask the students: "Do any of these names have anything in common?" (Answer: "They all begin with **čháŋ**.") Ask:

"What do you think **čháŋ** means?" (Answer: "tree/wood.")
"What does **čhaŋwápe** mean?" (Answer: "tree leaf/leaves."
"What do you think **kasná** means?" (Answer: "The sound wind makes (in the trees/leaves).");
"What do you think **napȟópa** means?" (Answer: " popping sound that trees make when it is very cold.");
"Why do you think these months are named in this way?"
Continue with the other months using a similar strategy questions and hints, such as:
Ištáwičhayazaŋ Wí {March} = "The moon of sore eye (Answer: "The sun's reflection on the snow causes sn blindness.") The students should already know **ištá** {eye **Wičháyazaŋ** means "they hurt."
Thíŋpsiŋla Itkáȟča Wí {June} = "The moon when turr are in blossom." (Ask "What happens to turnip plants June… look at the picture"…; "What does **itkáȟča** mean?"
Wasútȟuŋ Wí {August} = "The moon of ripeness."
Waníyetu Wí {November} = "The winter moon (wi begins)."
Tȟahé Kapšúŋ Wí {December} = "The moon when c shed their antlers." (also pronounced **Tȟahéčapšuŋ tȟahé** {horns, antlers}, **kapšúŋ** {to throw down}).
Wiótheȟika Wí {January} = "The moon when the su scarce"; **wí** {sun}, **theȟíka** {scarce} **wí** {moon}.

- **Weather**

Have the children look at the weather images along the e of the Lesson Page. Have them figure out what the indivi words mean. Practice pronunciation.

- **Owáštečake naíŋš Ošíčečake**

You may divide the weather terms into two gro **owáštečake** {good/pleasant weather} and **ošíčečake** { unpleasant weather}. Have the children help you place weather terms in two groups.

- **Seasons**

Ask the children to look at the four large pictures and fi out which seasons they illustrate. Ask them to read Lakota names for the seasons. Teach them the pr pronunciation and help them memorize the words additional activities.

Tell the students that you will say names of months and should respond with the appropriate season, as
T: **Wasútȟuŋ wí**. ➔ S: **blokétu**. etc. (Use the picture d this activity.) Then try matching weather terms with seas

- **Tȟatúye Tópa**

Using questions and hints, help the students find out wha four words in the inner circle mean (four directions). questions like: "Which direction does winter come fr (Answer: "North.") etc. In this way, connect the direc with the seasons. At the end, explain that each seasor direction has its own color. If your community uses diff colors, you may ask the children to draw, color and glu circular sectors over the image.

- **Seasons and Directions**

Name a season or direction (or even a month) and hav students say the appropriate color.

upížata

zíčá

halháta / uŋkčékhiȟa

hiŋháŋ

igmútȟaŋkc

matȟó

heȟáka

ȟoká

šuŋǧíla

itȟúŋkasaŋ

kȟaŋǧí

tȟažúška

wičhítegleǧa

tȟašnáheča

1. Color the animals and find their Lakota names.

ičá, šuŋǧíla, heȟáka, hiŋháŋ, wičhítegleǧa, upížata, halháta (uŋkčékhiȟa),
mútȟaŋka, kȟaŋǧí, itȟúŋkasaŋ, matȟó, tȟažúška, tȟašnáheča, ȟoká.

abulary and notes on pg. 108. Use the same instructions as Unit 13 *On the Plains*, pg. 54.

thuswéčha

hoyázela

čhapȟúŋka

siŋkpȟé

blóza

čhápa

pȟatkáša

gnaška

hoǧáŋ

matúška

Vocabulary on pg. 108. Use the same instructions as Unit 13, *On the Plains*, pg. 54.

Classroom Activities – Flashcard Methods

Flashcard methods are an essential component of this textbook. The textbook itself should be used to reinforce the knowledge gained by flashcards activities and especially to provide opportunities for recognizing or reading Lakota words. Flashcard activities are lively and retain children's attention for a much longer time than working with a textbook alone.

Flashcard Activities to Introduce New Vocabulary

The number of flashcards used for introducing new vocabulary items will depend upon two factors, the age of the children and their knowledge of the language. With young beginners, sets of 6 to 8 flashcards are recommended (up to 12 can be used for review activities). For older or more advanced students you can use up to 14 cards.

Flashcard activities are either passive or active. The passive are focused on children's ability to recognize words (aurally or visually). The active expect the students to use the words or sentences themselves. The teaching and learning process should go from passive to active.

1. See and Pronounce

- Take out a set of new vocabulary flashcards (6–8).
- Show the flashcards one by one to the children and say the Lakota words.
- Children as a group repeat after you.

2. Point at a Card (Passive Knowledge of Vocabulary)

- Place 6 to 12 previously introduced flashcards around the classroom.
- Say Lakota words and have the children point at the proper flashcards.
- (Optionally, allow the children to go to the card and bring it to you or to their desk depending on the needs of your next activity.)
- With more advanced students, use sentences, such as: **Šúŋka waŋ makípazo wo!** {Show me a dog!} or **Šúŋka kiŋ tuktél úŋ hwo/he?** {Where is the dog?}.

3. The Disappearing Card (Active)

This activity is very effective for practicing or reviewing vocabulary. Children usually enjoy it very much.

- Place up to 10 previously-introduced vocabulary flashcards on the board.
- Have the children say the Lakota words in the order in which the cards are on the board.

- Take one of the cards away and let the children say all the words again, including the missing card.
- Continue taking cards away as long as the children can say all the words in their original order.

The same activity can be used with written words instead of flashcards. This technique is used to practice the written form of the words. However, this version is much less enjoyable, especially for young children.

4. Missing Card

- Place about 6 to 8 flashcards on the board.
- Have the children turn around. (**Okáwiŋǧ po/pe!**) Take one of the flashcards away.
- Have the students say the word (or description) of the missing card.

5. A New Card

- Place about 8 to 10 flashcards on the board.
- Have the children turn around or close their eyes (**Ištógmuza po/pe!**). Replace one of the flashcards with a different flashcard.
- Have the students say the word (or description) of the new card. Continue with other cards.

6. Connecting Words to Flashcards

- Place up to 20 previously-introduced flashcards on the board.
- One by one, show the children the written Lakota words for the displayed items.
- Call on individual children to take a written word and put it above the appropriate flashcard.

7. Number the Flashcard

This is an efficient activity for teaching numbers and it is useful for introducing or practicing new vocabulary after numbers are learned.

- Put a set of flashcards on the board (up to 10) and number them.
- Say any Lakota number from 1 to 10 and have the children say the Lakota word under that number.
- Reverse the activity. Say the word and have the children say the numbers.

8. Modifier Versus Noun (or Noun Versus Verb)

This activity is useful for practicing modifiers (colors, sizes) as well as verbs.

- Put a set of flashcards on the board.
- Say the color (or other modifier) and have children say the noun.
- Then say the noun and the children say the color.

- For verbs, say the verb and have the children say the noun.
- Say the noun and have the children say the verb.
- At the end, ask the children to say both the noun and modifier (or noun and verb).

. If True, Clap Your Hands!

Show a set of flashcards one by one to the children.

If you say the correct word for it, the children should clap their hands, if incorrect they remain silent.

This activity can be altered in many ways. For example, you can add a modifier like **šúŋka sápa** or a verb, like **šúŋka kiŋ íŋyaŋke**. Children enjoy it thoroughly.

Comment: Clapping hands is effective with young children (1ˢᵗ to 6ᵗʰ grade) because it keeps them active and employs their kinesthetic memory. With older students, you may want to replace clapping with a verbal response, such as **Háŋ** {Yes} vs. **Hiyá** {No} or **Wičákȟe** {True} vs. **Wičákȟe šni** {False}, **Wičáyakȟe** {You are right.} vs. **Wičáyakȟe šni** {You are not right.}.

0. Odd One Out! (Active)

Select 4 to 6 flashcards of the same lexical class, such as animals, toys, and numbers. Include one card that is not in the same lexical set as the others.

Hold up each card in turn and have the children say the name of the item. When you show the card that does not belong, have the children call out, "Odd one out!" (or in Lakota, e.g.: **Ópȟa šni!** {Doesn't belong!})

Repeat with different sets of cards.

. What is the Opposite?

Have the children say the word expressing the opposite of the item on the flashcard you show them. (Examples: man-woman, dog-cat, large-small, black-white etc.)

. Lip Reading

Place 6 to 10 flashcards on the board.

Point at one and mouth the word without making any sound.

Have the children look at your lips as you mouth the word and guess what you are saying.

Try repeating the same activity without pointing at the flashcards.

13. Copy Me!

- Hold up a flashcard and say the word. Ask children to copy you.
- Say the word again, this time very softly. Have the children repeat the word softly.
- Say the word in varying ways, such as loudly, slowly, quickly, sadly, angrily. Each time, have the children copy the way you say it.

(This activity feels like a game for children. It is very useful for memorizing the proper pronunciation of words. Do the activity for max. 5 minutes.)

14. Guess the Card, Children!

- Show any 6 previously-learned flashcards to the children.
- Remove one of the flashcards without letting the children see which one you have.
- Have them guess the card by saying a sentence like:
- **Hé wówapi héčha hwo/he?** (make sure you only call on one child at a time).
- If the guess is not correct, say: **Hiyá, hé wówapi héčha šni.**
- If a child guesses the word correctly, nod your head yes and say: **Háŋ, hé wówapi héčha.**
- Play this game 3 or 4 times, with different sets of flashcards.
- Optionally, allow the child who guessed correctly to pick a card and answer the questions.

15. Guess the Card, Teacher!

- Show a set of 6 to 8 flashcards to the class.
- Place them in a pile face down in front of you. Take one card from the middle of the pile and place it on the bottom without looking at it.
- Flip the pile over with the bottom card facing the children so that they can see the picture, but you can't.
- Ask them **Lé [šúŋka] héčha hwo/he?**
- The children answer like this: **Hiyá, hé [šúŋka] héčha šni.** You should keep guessing until you are correct and then say **Háŋ, hé [šúŋka] héčha.** (With some classes you may only be able to use **háŋ** and **hiyá**.)

Note: Avoid using a single word (e.g. **šúŋka**) to guess the card. These activities allow a wide variety of questions, such as, **Hé [wówapi] héčha hwo/he?** or **Wówapi waŋží bluhá hwo/he?** etc.

16. What's Next?

- Show a set of 6 to 8 flashcards and show them to the class.
- Shuffle the flashcards and place them in a pile face down in front of you.
- Call on a child and ask, **Táku ihákab yá hwo/he?** or **Táku ókihaŋ hwo/he?** {What's next?}. The child has to guess the card before you turn it over. You can make a guess too.
- Then turn over the card to see who was right.
- If you guess correctly, you score a point, and if the child guesses correctly the class scores a point.

17. Little by Little

- Choose a flashcard, cover it with a piece of another card and hold it up for the class to see.
- Move the covering card a few inches down, revealing the card below. Ask: **Lé táku hwo/he?**
- Children answer with a guess, e.g.: **Hé gnašká héčha.**
- Allow a few more inches of the card to be moved and ask again: **Lé táku hwo/he?**
- Children guess again, e.g.: **Hé oákaŋke héčha.**
- Keep revealing a bit more of the flashcard until children guess the picture.

18. Bring a Card, a Team Game

- Divide the class into two teams.
- Have each team stand in a line behind a desk covered with the 10 upturned flashcards. Both teams have the same cards.
- At the start of each round have one member of each team approach the desk.
- As the teacher says a word or phrase, such as **Šúŋka sápe,** the students must choose which card matches the phrase.
- The first student who brings the correct flashcard to the board wins a point for his/her team. If you want to avoid running, allow the children to simply show the flashcard.

19. Alphabetical Order

- Distribute 6 to 8 flashcards to the children (or to two groups of them) and have them line up alphabetically according to what card each individual child has.
- (Choose the items carefully. First have the children become familiar with the order of the Lakota alphabet, which includes the special characters with diacritics.)

20. Guess the Color

- Choose an animal or an object and tell the children the Lakota word for it, like: **kimímela wíyatke** etc.
- Then tell them that you have its color in your mind and that they must guess the color by asking like this: **Kimímela zí.**
- Teacher answers: **Hiyá, zí šni.** or **Háŋ, zí.**
- Alternatively, have the child who guessed correctly do your job.

21. Guess the Color, Children!

- Show 6 to 8 flashcards of things, clothing, animals to the children and have them memorize the words using: **Lená kiksúya po/pe!** {Memorize them}.
- Put the flashcards in a pile. Look at one of them (without showing it to the children) and ask them:
- **Wówapi kiŋ oówa tókča hwo/he?** {What color is the book?}
- The children answer: **Wówapi kiŋ tȟózi.**
- Continue with the other flashcards.

22. Guess the Color, Teacher!

- Choose 6 different flashcards and repeat the previous activity. This time, you need to try to remember the color of the items and have the children ask you about them.
- The children ask: **Wówapi kiŋ oówa tókča hwo/he?**

23. Who has what?

- Have the children, each with a flashcard, form a circle (You may gesture and say **Yumímeya ináži po/pe!**).
- Be part of the circle. Put your flashcard on the floor in front of you and signal the children to do the same (at the same time you can say: **Khúta égnaka po/pe!**).
- Have the children clap their hands, if you say a correct sentence. Say sentences like:
- **David zuzéča waŋ yuhá. / Tina tȟatȟáŋka waŋ yuhá.** etc.
- Later you can make it more difficult mentioning the colors as well, e.g.:
- **Peter kimímela ská waŋ yuhá.** {Peter has a white butterfly.}

24. Kiŋ + Oówa tókča; Guess the Color, Teacher!

- Have the children turn their flashcards over so that the blank side up.
- Teacher says: **Ógle.**
- The student who has the flashcard of a shirt raises his/her hand and asks you this way:

Ógle kiŋ oówa tókča hwo/he?

Teacher answers: Ógle kiŋ ȟóta.

The child shows the flashcard. If the teacher's guess is correct, all the children clap their hands.

Note that when asking about animals híŋtokča is used instead: Šúŋka kiŋ lé híŋtokča hwo/he? {What color is the dog? / What hair color does the dog have?}.

5. Plurals

Use flashcards illustrating items in both singular and plural. The children find both cards and say:

Lé gnašká héčha. Lená gnašká héčhapi. (animate objects)

Lé wóžuha héčha. Lená wóžuha héčha. (inanimate objects)

This activity is good for practicing hé/lé versus lená/lená as well as for practicing héčhapi (for animate objects) and héčha (for plural of inanimate objects).

6. Matching Games

You can match different sorts of flashcards, such as animals and what they eat (šúŋkawakȟáŋ – peží), animals and where they live (hoǧáŋ – mní).

This can produce short sentences like "The frog is in the pond." "The fish is in the river." and so on.

7. Collecting and Grouping Cards

Have the children group the flashcards into sets like people, animals, clothes, food, etc.

Alternatively, give each child a card and have him/her find a classmate who has a card belonging to the same set (animals, clothes etc).

8. Spelling Game

(Only for older students where Lakota writing has begun.)

Divide the class into two teams, A and B. Put a flashcard on the board. Choose a child from Team A to come and write the word on the board next to the card. Award one point if the child identifies the object correctly, and one point for the correct spelling. Then choose another flashcard and ask a child from Team B to come and write the word. The team with the most points at the end is the winner.

9. Stop

Take six flashcards. Say a word and then show the children the flashcards one by one. As soon as they see the card which matches the word you said, they call out Ináǧiŋ! (Stop!)

30. What's Your Card?

- Take five or six lexical sets of flashcards, such as food, clothes, and animals.
- Call on an individual child to come to your desk and give him or her a flashcard. Explain that they must not show it to anyone.
- After each child has a flashcard explain that they must find children with cards in the same lexical set as their own.
- Children walk around the class asking each other Táku (čha) luhá hwo/he? When they have found all the members of their set they sit down.

31. How many cards can you remember?

- Put ten to sixteen flashcards on the board.
- Have the children look at the cards for two minutes. Remove them and ask the children to write down as many words as they can remember.

32. Memory (Find the Pair)

Lay a set of picture and word cards face down on a table. The players turn over two cards in each turn. If they find a pair, they can take the cards. If they do not find a pair, they must turn the cards over again and leave them there. This game increases language skills and improves awareness of spatial relationships. It should be played with smaller cards (not with the large flashcards). There are three main variants of the game:

1) Each item is represented by two identical cards with pictures. The players play the game in groups of four and have them turn over two cards in each turn. If they find a pair, they take the cards and score a point, but they have to say the Lakota word for the pair. Otherwise, they must turn the cards over again in their original place.

2) Each item is represented by two cards. One has a picture, the other a word in Lakota. Players play the game in groups of four and have them turn over two cards in each turn. If they find a pair, they take the cards and score a point. Otherwise they turn the cards over again in their original position.

3) Each item is represented by two identical cards with pictures and a word. One of the cards has the word in English, the other in Lakota. The players play the game in groups of four and they turn over two cards at each turn. If they turn over a card with the English word, they have to say the Lakota word and vice versa. If they find a pair, they take the cards and score a point, but they have to say the proper words. Otherwise, they turn the cards over again in their original position.

Oral Vowels

a	like 'a' in *father*	sápa, na, šá, ská, kál, sutá
e	like 'e' in *bed*	hél, lél, hená, éna, ehé, wewé, heyé
i	like 'i' in *machine*	iná, líla, zí, nípi, thí, thípi, níča
o	like 'o' in *soft*	oná, oní, wóze, olé, žožó, okó, yeló
u	like 'u' in *tune*	úpi, aú, hú, húta, huhú, sú, yuhá

Nasal vowels

aŋ	like 'o' in *money*, nasalized	aŋpétu, toháŋ, čhaŋkú, waŋží
iŋ	like 'i' in *mink*, nasalized	íŋkpa, íŋyaŋ, khiŋíŋ, wíŋyaŋ
uŋ	like 'oo' in *moon*, nasalized	úŋyaŋ, uŋspé, kaúŋka, nakúŋ, múŋ

examples

Fricatives			
	s	like 's' in *so*	sí, sápa, misúŋkala
	š	like 'sh' in *shop*	šúŋka, hokšíla
	s'	like s followed by the glottal stop	míyoglas'iŋ,
	š'	like š followed by the glottal stop	š'éš'e,
	z	like 'z' in *zero*	zí, zičá, záptaŋ
	ž	like 'z' in *azure*	waŋží, wóžuha
	ǧ	like the French or German 'r'	ǧí, šaglóǧaŋ, ǧú
	ȟ	close to Spanish x in Mexico	ȟóta, ȟé, wičháȟpi, heȟáka
	ȟ'	like ȟ followed by the glottal stop	wičhóȟ'aŋ

Continuants			
	h	like 'h' in *hat*	hí, hú, sihá
	w	like 'w' in *was*	wí, wówapi
	y	like 'y' in *yoke*	yuhá, yámni
	l	like 'l' in *lap*	luhá, lé, misúŋkala
	m	like 'm' in *map*	máza, yámni
	n	like 'n' in *nap*	núŋpa, natá, šni

Stops

The proper pronunciation and writing of the three different types of stops is essential for determining the meaning of Lakota words (cf. How to teach stops on page 96.).

) Plain Stops (This is the most frequent type of stop in Lakota, up to **75%** of all stops.)

č	no equivalent in English, (but close to 'ch' in *rich*)	wíčazo, ptéčela, ečíyapi, čónala, ičú
k	like 'k' in *skin*	šúŋka, wíyatke, kimímela, kiŋ, šakówiŋ, táku
p	like 'p' in *spin* or in *happy*	tópa, šákpe, pispíza, napíŋkpa, po, ípuza
t	like 't' in *still*	táku, até, maštíŋčala, tópa, tuwé

Aspirated Stops (These represent about 23% of all stops in Lakota.)[1]

A) Aspirated stops with strong (or guttural) aspiration (about 15% of all stops)

The strong (or guttural) aspiration is not marked in most printed documents, because there are local and individual variations. However, teachers are encouraged to mark strong aspiration in writing whenever they feel it appropriate. This is particularly helpful for beginning students. In most communities the strong aspiration generally occurs before **a, aŋ, o, uŋ**.

kȟ	no equivalent in English	kȟáta, kȟáŋta, kȟó, kȟuŋšítku
pȟ	no equivalent in English	pȟáta, scépȟaŋ, napȟópa, čapȟúŋka
tȟ	no equivalent in English	mitȟáwa, tȟáŋka, tȟó, tȟuŋkášila

B) Aspirated stops with soft aspiration (about 8% of all stops)

čh	like 'ch h' in *much haste*	čháŋ, čheží, čhiyé, čhowíŋža, čhuŋkší, čhíŋ
kh	like 'kh' in *khaki* (the color)	khíza, akhé, khúža, khúl, khuwá, akhí, pakhíŋta
ph	like 'p h' in *steep hill*	íphi, phuté, nuphíŋ, aphíya
th	like 't h' in *sit here*	thí, thušú, thebyá, wathí, thíŋpsiŋla

Ejective Stops (stops followed by glottal stops; only about 2% of stops in Lakota)

č'	like 'ch' followed by a glottal stop	kič'úŋ, ič'íč'u, nič'ú, mnič'ápi, šič'é
k'	like 'k' followed by a glottal stop	k'ú, ok'ó, k'á, ok'é, k'íŋ, k'uŋ
p'	like 'p' followed by a glottal stop	op'ó, p'é, wanáp'iŋ, kap'óža
t'	like 't' followed by a glottal stop	nat'á, kat'é, nat'íŋza, čhet'úŋgla, ot'ógnaka

---

...ps have **soft aspiration** before **i, iŋ, u**; and **strong aspiration** before **a, aŋ, o, uŋ**. Individual speakers and communities have ...ing habits on aspiration before **e**, thus both types of aspiration can occur before **e**. However, whenever 'e' is the result of the ...ge from 'a' or 'aŋ', it is preceded by strong aspiration (e.g. **epȟé ló**). The same rule is applied for 'iŋ' (**epȟíŋ kte**).

When teaching kindergarteners, it is best to avoid explaining pronunciation. Teachers and parents should instead rely fully on demonstration and repetition. Beginning with the first grade, the number of targeted pronunciation exercises should slowly increase. Children like imitating sounds and are very good at it. Therefore, if the activities are playful enough, children will have no problem learning new sounds.

At the early elementary levels, the goal should be to teach passive knowledge of Lakota spelling. This means that the sounds of individual letters as well as the pronunciation of syllables should be recognized. They need not be required to write words on their own or without guidance. The exercises are aimed at the students' recognition of sounds and sometimes their ability to read Lakota words, but not at their active writing in Lakota.

By grade four teachers may start providing more exercises involving active usage of written Lakota. Because the Lakota language is spelled consistently, it is much easier to write than English. Thus, a passive knowledge on the K-3 level is often a sufficient basis for later literacy in Lakota beginning with grade 4. It is not important that the words used in pronunciation exercises be learned as vocabulary items. They are for studying the sounds only. For now, their meaning is not important. Some of the words in the exercises are rare and the children do not need to know them at this point. On some occasions we will also use individual syllables that are not words at all.

Unit 1. Oral Vowels (a, e, i, o, u)

Before the lesson, produce handouts by creating sheets with the Lakota vowels on them. Have the children cut these five vowels out of the sheets.
Write the five oral vowels on the board: a e i o u. Ask the children to repeat them after you: a e i o u.

Then say the vowels in the following syllables (choose at random). Children should repeat each syllable and at the same time raise a card with the appropriate vowel.

ba, ha, la, wa, ya	sa, za, (ša, ža, ča)
be, he, le, we, ye	se, ze, (še, že, če)
bi, hi, li, wi, yi	si, zi, (ši, ži, či)
bo, ho, lo, wo, yo	so, zo, (šo, žo, čo)
bu, hu, lu, wu, yu	su, zu, (šu, žu, ču)

Vowels should be taught in syllables above (they are formed with consonants that have the same or similar

pronunciation in Lakota as in English). The syllable in parentheses should only be practiced orally because š, ž and č have not yet been introduced.

Unit 2: Plain stops (č, k, p, t)

Plain stops are among the most common Lakot consonants, but are extremely rare in English. (In fac most English speakers don't even hear the sound o plain stops unless trained for it). Therefore, proper an consistent practice of their pronunciation at an earl stage of learning Lakota is essential. It is important t teach Lakota plain stops before teaching aspirate stops, whose pronunciation is closer to most Englis stops. Plain stops are introduced in Unit 2.

- Write these English words on the board: **kin, pi till**. Read the words to the children (or ask them read the words if they are in reading age).
- Take a sheet of paper, hold it at the upper marg and place it in front of your mouth. Stand sideways the children and say the words "**kin**," "**pin**," "**till**."
- Ask the children: "What happened to the pap when I said those English words?"
- The children should respond with something li "It moved."
- Teacher: "Try it yourself. Take a sheet of pap and say these words."
- Teacher explains: "The sheet of paper mov because there is a puff of air following the letters **k,** and **t** in the English words."
- Teacher: "A few English words don't have t puff of air, for instance: skin, spin, still. Try it yours and see that the paper is no longer moving."
- Teacher: "Most k's, p's, t's in Lakota don't ha this puff of air. We have to practice saying the letters without it. Let's practice, repeat after me:"
- **ská, skúya, kíza, oákaŋke; ištá, is táku, tóna, tuwé, itówapi; spáya, páp púza, pispíza**
- Use a similar approach to explain that the sa difference exists between English **ch** (as in chair) Lakota **č** (many č's in Lakota are without the puff air). Practice it saying these words:
- **čónala, wíčazo, tókča, wakší hokšíčala, zuzéča, zičá, šíčá, i winúŋčala**
- With young students it is recommended introduce one stop at a time, in this order: **k, p, t, č**

Create handouts for children to cut out little cards with [, k, p, t. Then say the words above at random. The children should repeat and raise the appropriate cards.

Note for teachers: To an untrained English ear the Lakota plain stops **k, p, t, č** sound like the English [, **b, d, j**. For example the Lakota word **táku** seems to sound like "**dágu**" or the word **čónala** like "**jónala**." These two sets of sounds may seem similar to English speakers, but in reality, they are different. The best way to practice the proper pronunciation of Lakota plain stops is to have the students try to imitate the stops in s<u>k</u>in, s<u>p</u>in, s<u>t</u>ill. You can expect that your students may pronounce **k, p, t, č** as **g, b, d, j** in the beginning. Encourage them positively if they do and make them repeat after you as frequently as possible. Mastering the pronunciation of plain stops is one of the most important things about learning the Lakota language.

Unit 3: Nasal Vowels (aŋ, iŋ, uŋ)

The three vowels: **aŋ, iŋ, uŋ** are called "nasals" because the air passes through both the nose and the mouth when they are pronounced. Children should not have problems learning to express these sounds if you give them enough time and opportunity to practice. Write **aŋ** on the board and have the children repeat these words after you:

aŋ: waŋ, aŋpétu, sáŋ, háŋ, waŋží, yaŋká

Do the same with **iŋ** and **uŋ**:

iŋ: íŋyaŋ, íŋkpa, wíŋyaŋ, nážiŋ, wakíŋyaŋ

uŋ: uŋčí, úŋpi, nakúŋ, uŋyúha, iyúŋka

Remind students to identify these letter combinations **aŋ, iŋ, uŋ** as one sound each.

Unit 4: Lakota sounds ȟ and ǧ

Lakota letters **ȟ** and **ǧ** are sometimes referred to as gutturals. They are marked with a dot in some writing systems. The LLC orthography employs the wedge in order to use as few diacritics as possible throughout the writing system. The wedge is also easier to see.

Children will be able to pronounce these sounds easily by imitating their teacher or the audio CD.

Write the letters on the board and have the children repeat the following words:

ȟ: ȟóta, ȟé, ȟá, húŋȟ, ȟwá, waȟčá, ȟló, ȟla, waȟpé, ȟoká

ǧ: ǧí, ǧú, ǧáŋ, maǧá, káǧe, šaglóǧaŋ, ǧiǧí, maǧa, ǧópa, ǧépa

Practice **ȟ** and **ǧ** in syllables:

ȟ: ȟa, ȟe, ȟi, ȟo, ȟu, ȟaŋ, ȟiŋ, ȟuŋ

ǧ: ǧa, ǧe, ǧi, ǧo, ǧu, ǧaŋ, ǧiŋ, ǧuŋ

Ideally, work with the flashcards of these syllables. Write **ǧ** and **ȟ** on the left and right hand sides of the board and ask the children to point at the letter they hear. Then say the words above, picking words with **ǧ** and **ȟ** at random.

Make a comparison of **h** versus **ȟ** and **g** versus **ǧ** with the appropriate exercises. Have the children point at the proper side of the board or show the flashcard etc.

Note: The letter **ǧ** only appears before vowels (**ǧa, ǧe, ǧi, ǧo, ǧu, ǧaŋ, ǧiŋ, ǧuŋ**).

Unit 5: kȟ, kh

The sounds **kȟ** and **kh** are aspirated stops. Aspirated stops are much more infrequent than plain stops (**k**). Still, being able to differentiate aspirated stops from plain stops is essential for learning correct pronunciation and understanding. It is important to start teaching aspirated stops with **kȟ** and **kh**, because these digraphs don't occur in English (unlike **ph** and **th**). Once the children understand the concept of reading and pronouncing **kȟ** and **kh** they will easily transfer this concept to **pȟ, ph** and **tȟ, th**.

• Review the pronunciation of plain stops and make sure the children are very familiar with them before you start teaching **kȟ, kh**. Write **k** on the left hand side of the board and ask the children:
• "Do you remember how this Lakota sound differs from the English one?"
• Their answer should be similar to this: "It doesn't have the puff of air (following it)."
• Praise the children if they give you the correct answer. Encourage and help them with hints if they can't recall. If needed, repeat the demonstration with the sheet of paper in front of the mouth.
• Then say this: "Most Lakota **k**'s don't have this puff of air. But sometimes **k** is followed by the letter **ȟ**, which we have learned recently. Then we have **kȟ**."
• Have the children practice the pronunciation of **kȟ** by repeating these words after you or the CD:
kȟáta, kȟó, makȟá, kȟál, kȟuŋší, kȟáŋta

• Write **kȟ** on the board separately from **k** like this (don't write **kh** yet):

left side of the board	middle of the board	right side of the board
k	kȟ	kh

- Ask the children to listen and point at that side of the board with the letter they hear. Alternatively use small paper cards with the letters k, kȟ, kh – children raise the card with the sound they hear.
- Then read the following words (or play the CD) making a pause after each word for the children to point at the proper side of the board (or raise a card). Praise them with wašté after each proper response and repeat the word if some of the students react incorrectly:

šúŋka, nakúŋ, kȟáta, kȟó, maká, makȟá, kál, kȟál, kúŋza, kȟuŋší, kȟáŋta, kiŋ.

Then say: "Occasionally the letter k is followed by a puff of air just like in English. When that happens the puff of air is written as the letter h: kh." (Note: kh is the least frequent of these three k's)

Write kh on the right hand side of the board and say these words: khíza, khuté, khuwá, okhíse.

Then again ask the children to listen and point at the side of the board with the sound they hear:

khíza, kíza, nakúŋ, khúta, okhíse, okíhi, khuwá, maká, akhí, kiŋ, khiŋíŋ.

Then mix all three types together, children point at the left, middle or right hand side of the board:

šúŋka, khíza, nakúŋ, khúta, kȟáta, kíza, kȟó, maká, akhí, makȟá, kál, kȟál, kúŋza, kéye, kȟuŋší; khuwá.

Unit 6: tȟ, th

For teaching tȟ and th use the same strategy as in teaching kȟ, kh above. (Don't forget to review the pronunciation of plain t, as in táku.)

left side of the board	middle of the board	right side of the board
t	tȟ	th

For practicing pronunciation use these sets of words:

tȟ: tȟáŋka, tȟó, tȟuŋkášila, mitȟáŋkala, otȟúŋwahe, tȟaŋčháŋ, tȟáwa.

t versus tȟ: táku, tȟáŋka, tó, tȟó, tȟuŋkášila, mitȟáŋkala, tuŋwáŋ, otȟúŋwahe, tȟaŋčháŋ, tuwé, tȟáwa.

t versus th: tuwá, thušú, othí, ištíŋma, maštíŋčala, čhethí, thibló, tóna, thíŋta, thíŋpsila, táku.

Mix all of the words in the end.

Ask the children: "What is the difference between the pronunciation of 'th' in English and in Lakota?"

98

Children should be able to explain, help them i needed. Then write on the board:

English	Lakota
think	thípi
thank	tȟáŋka
that	tȟaté

Ask the children to point at that side of the board wit the word you say. Then ask them to say the words o their own.

The children may have a problem distinguishing th English and Lakota pronunciation of th in th beginning, but if the teacher provides enough practic the students will eventually learn the proper sound.

Unit 7: pȟ, ph

For teaching pȟ and ph use the same strategy as in teaching kȟ, kh above. (Don't forget to review the pronunciation of plain p, as in púza.)

left side of the board	middle of the board	right side of the board
p	pȟ	ph

For practicing pronunciation use these sets of words

pȟ: pȟasú, čhapȟúŋka, apȟé, napȟé, pȟehȟ
p versus pȟ: paksá, pȟasú, púza, čhapȟúŋk apȟé, napé, napȟé
p versus ph: ípi, íphi, phuté, púza, aphíya, napíŋkpa
Mix all of the words in the end.

Ask the children: "What is the difference between pronunciation of 'ph' in English and in Lakot Children should be able to explain, help them needed. Then write on the board:

English	Lakota
Phil	philá
phone	phóǧe

Ask the children to point at that side of the board v the word you say. Then ask them to say the words their own.

Don't worry too much if the children pronounce p [f] in the beginning. If you provide them v consistent practice of the pronunciation and encou them, they will learn to distinguish between English and Lakota pronunciation of ph.

Unit 8: č, čȟ

For teaching č and čȟ use the same strategy as in teaching kȟ, kh above. At first review the pronunciation of plain stops k, p, t. Then explain that also Lakota č often lacks the puff of air and that there is no such sound in English. Therefore the children have to try to omit the puff of air after č. You may tell the children that Lakota č sounds closer to the English sound "j", but it is not the same.

Practice č with these words: ičú, šíča, wíčazo, íča, ečéla, kačóčo.

left side of the board	right side of the board
č	čȟ

For practicing pronunciation use these sets of words:

š: šíča, kačóčo, ičú, zuzéča, wakšíča, zičá, ȟkča

versus čȟ: šíča, čȟáŋ, čȟóza, kačóčo, ȟuwíta, ičú, zuzéča, čȟápa, wakšíča, ȟetáŋ, zičá, tókča

Note: The difference between the sounds č and čȟ is sometimes difficult to hear even for adult native speakers. Don't be disappointed if the students struggle with this or if they tend to pronounce č as the English "j" at the beginning. Also, the sound čȟ does not occur in Lakota.

Unit 9: s, š and z, ž

Write the letter "s" on the board and ask the children to repeat the words below after you or the audio CD. Then do the same with words for š.

s: sápa, sí, sutá, misúŋka, oíse, sáŋ, séče, ŋté, sáka, sakhíb
š: šápa, ší, šíča, šéča, šúŋka, šákpe, wašté, ȟá, tȟaŋkší, hokšíla

Then say words with s or š at random and ask the children to repeat and raise the card with the appropriate letter.
Then do the same activity for z and ž:

z: zičá, záptaŋ, zí, zúŋta, ziŋtkála, ȟníyaŋ, zilyá, zíša
ž: žičá, žáta, ží, žaŋžáŋ, žíŋča, žožó, žúŋ, tȟakóža, nážiŋ,

In the end say the words for s, š, z, ž at random. The children should repeat and raise the appropriate cards.

Whenever the consonants s, š, z, ž appear at the beginning of a word, their pronunciation is a little bit longer than in English.

Unit 10: h, w, y, l, m, n

These Lakota consonants have the same or similar pronunciation as in English. Practice saying them in syllables like this:

ha, he, hi, ho, hu, háŋ, hiŋ, huŋ
wa, we, wi, wo, wu, waŋ, wiŋ
ya, ye, yi, yo, yu, yaŋ, yiŋ, yuŋ
la, le, li, lo, lu
ma, me, mi, mo, mu
na, ne, ni, no, nu

Unit 11: Ejective Stops

Ejective stops are very infrequent (only about 2% of stops in a text). They are written with the letter for the stop and for a glottal stop marked by an apostrophe ('). The glottal stop is a sharp closing of the glottis. Let the children repeat after you or the audio CD:

k': k'á, k'é, k'íŋ, k'ú, k'o
p': p'á, p'é, p'í, p'ó, p'u
t': t'á, t'é, t'i, t'o, t'u
č': č'á, č'e, č'i, č'o, č'u

Write plain stops on one side of the board and glottalized stops on the other side. Then, say the following words and the children should point to the appropriate group (or raise cards with letters):

plain: tuwá, nakúŋ, napé, čónala, táku, maká, púza, čočó, tópa, pazó, kiskíza
glottalized: t'á, ak'íŋ, p'ó, kič'á, t'uŋgyá, nap'íŋ, kič'úŋ, t'óza, k'uŋháŋ, p'é, šič'éši

Unit 12: Voiced Clusters: bl, gm, gn, gl, mn

Lakota speakers add a little "uh" sound (called a schwa, or a consonant release) between the two sounds to help go from one to the next. The release is never written, but the children will learn to pronounce it if they frequently hear and practice it.
Ask the children to repeat after you (or after the CD):
blé, bló, bluhá, ibláble, waŋblí, gmigmá, igmú, wagmíza, gnašká, gní, glá, glé, gló, ógle, gluhá, wígli, mní, wikčémna, yámni, yamnúmnuǧa.

99

Unit 13: Glottal Stop

We have already seen the glottal stop that occurs after
č, k, p and **t**. It also frequently follows the Lakota
sounds: **ȟ, s, š**. Write these on the left hand side,
middle and right hand side of the board (**ȟ', s', š'**).
Then demonstrate and practice pronunciation of one
of the three at a time:

ȟ': ȟ'áŋ, oȟ'áŋ, naȟ'úŋ, akíȟ'aŋ, iȟ'é,
ȟ'eȟ'é, kaȟ'ól, ȟ'okȟá, ȟ'úŋyaŋ, oyúȟ'i

s': s'á, kas'á, kas'íŋ, s'e, oyús'o, oyás'iŋ,
as'íŋ, nas'ós'o, yas'ós'o

š': š'á, š'é, waš'áka, yuš'íŋš'iŋ,
yuš'íŋyeya, iš'óš'o, onáš'oš'o, wíš'oš'o,

Units 14-23: Consonant Clusters

Below is a full list of consonant clusters that occur in
the Lakota language (with the exception of **bl, gm, gn,
gl, mn** which were dealt with in the previous unit).
Practice the pronunciation of these clusters in:

**gw, gy, ȟč, ȟl, ȟm, ȟn, ȟp, ȟt, ȟw, kč, kp, ks, kš, kt,
pč, ps, pš, pt, sč, sk, sl, sm, sn, sp, st, sw, šk, šl, šm,
šn, šp, št, šw, tk.**

Practice these consonant clusters in syllables with the
five oral vowels (e.g. **sma, sme, smi, smo, smu)**.
Clusters composed of two stops (**kč, kp, kt, pč, pt, tk**)
are going to be among the most difficult for the
children. You may need to give them extra time to
practice them. Clusters with **s, š** or **č** as their second
member, like: **ȟč, kč, ks, kš, pč, ps, pš, sč**, might also
be a challenge for some children.

Ask the children to repeat the words with these
clusters. With older or more advanced classes, you can
ask students to raise cards with letters to indicate the
combination of consonants. Practice only 3–4
consonant clusters per a lesson depending on the
children's progress.

1) **gw**: gwéza, nagwáka;
2) **gy**: sagyé, waš'ágya;
3) **ȟč**: ȟčiȟčí, waȟčá, ȟče;
4) **ȟl**: kaȟlí, siŋtéȟla, paȟlóka;
5) **ȟm**: theȟmúǧa, ȟmí, ináȟma;
6) **ȟn**: ináȟni, waȟná, kaȟníǧa;
7) **ȟp**: kaȟpá, maȟpíya, yuȟpá;
8) **ȟt**: ȟtayétu, yaȟtáka, pȟaȟtá;
9) **ȟw**: ȟwá, kaȟwóka, kaȟwá;
10) **kč**: kakčá, iyúkčaŋ, wikčémna;

11) **kp**: kakpá, čhekpá, kpazó;
12) **ks**: ksápa, ksízeča, kaksá;
13) **kš**: wakšíča, kšú, kšikšáŋ;
14) **kt**: kté, ktaŋktáŋ, yuktáŋ;
15) **pč**: napčá, napčíyuŋka, epčá;
16) **ps**: psáka, psíča, kapsíŋta;
17) **pš**: pšuŋkȟá, kapšúŋ, napšíža;
18) **pt**: pté, naptá, anáǧoptaŋ;
19) **sč**: čísčila, sčépȟaŋ, sčú;
20) **sk**: ská, skumná, skiskíta;
21) **sl**: slolyá, sloháŋ, slí;
22) **sm**: smí, smáka, čhasmú;
23) **sn**: snasná, snáza, sní, kasní, asní;
24) **sp**: spáŋla, spáya, spéya;
25) **st**: stáka, stóla, stostó, stustá;
26) **sw**: swaká, swúla, swuswúla;
27) **šk**: škáta, škáŋ, škečá, škiškná;
28) **šl**: šlá, šlašlá, šlí, šló;
29) **šm**: šmá, šmašmá, šmí, hiŋšmá;
30) **šn**: šná, yušná, šni, šníža;
31) **šp**: špáŋ, yušpí, yašpú;
32) **št**: štáka, štáŋ, yuštáŋ, kaštáŋ, hušté;
33) **šw**: šwéka, šwú, kašwú, wišwí;
34) **tk**: tká, tketké, tkúŋza

Standards for Written Lakota[2]

Every language has more than one style of speec
Style refers to the differences in speech in vario
situations. People usually speak differently in a form
setting than they do in a family environment. The tv
distinctive styles in Lakota are called **yat'íŋs
wóglaka** and **ikčéya wóglaka**. **Yat'íŋsya wóglaka**
a careful, formal speech in which every word
pronounced carefully and all the sounds are clea
articulated. **Ikčéya wóglaka** on the other hand i
style of casual, informal pronunciation. Slurri
omissions of certain sounds, and contractions of wo
are common.

It is usually the case that a standard for writ
language is based on the formal style of speech. I
example, in English people say, "I'm gonna go," or
gotta go." Yet, we write these expressions accord
to the slow pronunciation, like, "I am going to g
and, "I have got to go."

In Lakota we can also base the spelling of writ
language on **yat'íŋsya wóglaka**. This means that

---

[2] This section is largely based on a Lakota language study wr
by David Rood and Alan Taylor (Rood, D., Taylor, A.: La
Language Project, 1976, Colorado University, Boulder)
partly on the author's own research.

proper spelling of words should reflect the slow and careful pronunciation.

This does not mean, however, that the students should not learn **ikčéya wóglaka**. Teachers should introduce the fast speech forms to the children (they are often addressed in the teacher's guide) once the students are familiar with the formal pronunciation and spelling.

The following are the most frequent differences between **yat'íŋsya wóglaka** and **ikčéya wóglaka**. Teachers should study them carefully so that they spell and pronounce words according to the formal style.

Consonant h:

When the sound represented by "h" appears between vowels (e.g. **luhá**) it is often dropped in **ikčéya wóglaka**.

Here are some examples of words pronounced in careful versus slow speech:

Slow speech	Fast speech
luhá he?	luá e?
wahíŋkpe	waíŋkpe
haŋhépi	haŋépi
otȟúŋwahe	otȟúŋwae
óhuta	óuta
naháȟči	naáȟči
hóhotela	hóotela

Consonants w and y between two vowels:

Consonants **w** and **y** are pronounced in two different ways – strongly and weakly. In **yat'íŋsya wóglaka** (careful speech) they are strong, which means they sound just like in English. But in **ikčéya wóglaka** they become weak. In fact, they are so weak that they nearly disappear. Sometimes they actually do disappear. When this happens it changes the pronunciation of the neighboring vowels.

• Consonants **w** and **y** are always **strong** in the following cases:
– in slow and careful speech (**yat'íŋsya wóglaka**)
– in fast speech, if
• they are at the beginning of a word (**wakšíča, yašlé**)
• they follow a consonant (**š'agyá, slolyá**).

• Consonants **w** and **y** are always **weak** in fast speech when:
1) o, u, or uŋ comes before or after **w**.

2) e, i or iŋ comes before or after **y** (**y** usually isn't as weak as **w**).

w		y	
ú wo	úo	čhiyé	čhié
olówaŋ	olóaŋ	wíŋyaŋ	wíŋaŋ
owíŋža	oíŋža	ókiya	ókia
wówapi	wóapi	khéya	khéa

C) In fast speech, consonants **w** and **y** always disappear in the following combinations:
(1) -aya-, -eyé-, -aŋya-, aŋyaŋ-; (2) -owo-; (3) -aye-, -aŋye-; (4) awa-, -aŋwa-, -aŋwaŋ-, -awáŋ-,

The pronunciation of the weak **w** and **y**, or of the sound remaining after their disappearance depends on the surrounding vowels:

1) -aya- and -eye- are pronounced as a long Lakota **a** or **e** respectively *(double vowel stands for long vowel)*:

kéye	kéé
wašté yeló	waštéé ló
Slolyáya he?	Slolyáá he?
hayápi	háápi

If either or both of the surrounding a's are nasal, the long vowel is nasal too

waŋyáŋke	wááŋke

2) -owo- is pronounced as a long Lakota **o**:

owóte	óóte
abló wozáŋ	ablóózaŋ

3) -aye- is pronounced as a long vowel which sounds similar to the **a** in the English word "cab". The sound is nasalized if the preceding **a** is a nasal:

iyáye	iyǽ
philámayaye	philámayǽ
kitáŋyela	kitǽŋla
wakȟáŋyeža	wakȟǽŋža

4) -awa- is pronounced as a long vowel which sounds like the vowel at the beginning of "August", but with extra lip-rounding and the *au* in "audit". This sound is represented in the International Phonetic Alphabet (IPA) with "ɔ" and uses colon for marking a long vowel. The sound is nasalized if at least one of the a's is nasal:

mitȟáwa	mitȟǫ:
iyówawa	iyówǫ:
šúŋkawakȟáŋ	šúŋkǫ:kȟaŋ
wawáŋyaŋka	wǫ:ŋyaŋka

Suffix –pi before kta, kištó, na, kiŋ

The pronunciation of suffix –pi (plural) in fast speech before **kta**, **kištó/kštó**, **na** and **kiŋ** depends on the preceding vowels:

1) after **i** or **u**, the suffix is pronounced **u**:

Ípi kštó.	Íu kštó.
Lé ičúpi kte.	Lé ičúu kte.

2) after **iŋ** or **uŋ** the suffix is pronounced **uŋ**:

Naȟ'úŋpi kte.	Naȟ'úŋuŋ kte.
Khiŋíŋpi kte.	Khiŋíŋuŋ kte.

3) after **e** or **o**, the suffix is pronounced **o**:

Niwáštepi kštó.	Niwášteo kštó.
Ópi kte.	Óo kte.

4) after **a** or **aŋ**, the suffix is pronounced **o**, but the pronunciation of the vowel combinations **ao** and **aŋo** is merged:

Yápi kte.	Yáo kte.
Anáǧoptaŋpi kte.	Anáǧoptaŋo kte.
Iyáyapi kštó.	Iyááo kštó.

Suffix –pi before yeló, ye, yo

In both fast and slow speech the suffix –pi is merged with the following enclitics:
1) –pi + yeló = -pe ló:
   John emáčiyape ló. (never John emáčiyapi yeló.)
2) –pi + yo (male imperative) = po
   Anáǧoptaŋ po. (never Anáǧoptaŋpi yo.)
3) –pi + ye (female imperative) = pe
   Ú pe. (never Úpi ye.)

Note that the combination –pi + ye does occur unmerged, but in such case ye is not a female imperative, but an enclitic of polite command used by both men and women, as in: Akhé úpi ye. {Please, come again.}

Suffix –pi before he

In fast speech, the suffix -pi is contracted to –b when it comes before the question enclitic he:

   Táku eníčiyapi he?   Tág eníčiyab he?

Combination of nasal vowel and p or b.

When one of the nasal vowels (**aŋ**, **iŋ**, **uŋ**) comes before **p** or **b**, then they are fused together in fast speech and the results sounds like **m**:

correct spelling	fast speech
háŋpa	hámpa
waŋblí	wamblí
thíŋpsiŋla	thímpsiŋla (or thímsiŋla)
haŋblé	hamblé

Intervocalic Glottal Stop

A glottal stop is a sharp stop of the air-flow. It is th[e] sound represented by "-" in English **uh-oh**. In Lako[ta] language glottal stop is traditionally marked by a[n] apostrophe.

In slow and careful Lakota speech, the glottal sto[p] occurs between every two vowels. But in fast speech is frequently dropped. See some of these examples:

slow speech	fast speech (correct spelling)
a'ú	aú
o'ówa	oówa
a'í	aí
ó'uŋkiyapi	óuŋkiyapi
na'íŋš	naíŋš

In some vowel combinations, **y** is pronounced in t[he] original place of glottal stop. In such cases, t[he] spelling both with and without **y** are correct:

slow speech	correct spelling	
i'ógnaka =>	iógnaka =>	iyógnaka
thi'óšpaye =>	thióšpaye =>	thiyóšpaye
čhe'úŋpa =>	čheúŋpa =>	čheyúŋpa

The LLC orthography does not mark intervoca[lic] glottal stops and therefore the correct spelling [of] words is without it. However, teachers sho[uld] pronounce it when they speak to students. This w[ay] the children will grasp the proper yat'íŋ[?] pronunciation and at the same time will be able [to] drop the intervocalic glottal stop in fast speech.

Other changes in fast speech

Numerous changes take place during fast speech that are hard to categorize. Merging, dropping and contracting syllables are common phenomena. Remember that in these cases, the proper spelling is the one that reflects the slow and careful speech.

slow speech	fast speech
íŋš eyá	iŋžeá / iŋžáŋ
Tákuni šíčiŋ kte šni.	Tágni šíčiŋ ktiš.
Táku ehápi he?	Tákehab he?

Glossary

. Napéuŋkičhiyuza kte! — Let Us Shake Hands!

David miyé yeló.	I am David.
číyapi	his/her name is
máčiyapi	my name is
níčiyapi	your name is
okšíla	boy
omákšila	I am a boy
ištó, kštó	women's gender ending
Lisa miyé kštó.	I am Lisa.
Matáŋyaŋ yeló/kštó.	I am fine.
itúwe he?	Who are you?
Táku eníčiyapi he?	What is your name?
ókša akhé.	See you again.
oníkheča he?	How are you?
oníktuka he?	How are you?
wičhíŋčala	girl
wimáčhiŋčala	I am a girl
eló	men's gender ending

Lé táku hwo/he? — What is this?

káŋwowapi	desk
e?	question enclitic
owapi	picture
úšla (wíyukse)	scissors
Lé táku hwo/he?	What is this?
Lé wówapi héčha.	This is a book.
kaŋke	chair
aŋbláska	board, black board
wakšíča	plate, bowl
čazo	pencil
yaskabye	glue
yatke	cup
uŋspe omnáye	computer
wowapi	book
wowapi ská	paper
žuha	bag
yópa	door

Tóna hwo/he? — How Many?

ŋží	one
ŋpa, núm	two
nni	three
a, tób	four
taŋ	five
pe	six

šakówiŋ	seven
šaglóğaŋ	eight
napčíyuŋka	nine
wikčémna	ten
akéwaŋži	eleven
akénuŋpa	twelve
Tóna he?	How many?
mázaškaŋškaŋ	clock, o'clock

4. Oówa Tókča he? — What color is it?

gnašká	frog
ğí	brown
ȟóta, ȟótA	gray
kimímila, kimímela	butterfly
oówa	color
sáŋ	dull white, whitish
sápa	black
ská	white
šá	red
šastáŋ	pink
tȟó	blue (green)
tȟósaŋ	light blue
tȟósapA	dark blue
tȟóša	purple
tȟózi	green (light green)
waȟčá	flower
wígmuŋke	rainbow
wíyaka, wíyake	feather
zí	yellow
zíša	orange
zíškopela, zíškopa	banana

5. Lé tókheča he? — What does it look like?

čík'ala	small
háŋskA	long
ičázopi	line
miméla	circle
oblótȟuŋ háŋska	rectangle
oblótȟuŋ	square
oíse-yámni	triangle
pȟéstola	diamond
ptéčela	short
tȟáŋkA	large, big
wičháȟpi	star

6. Wóškate   Toys

bluhá	I have
čhéǧa	kettle, bucket
haŋpóšpu	doll
hokšípaslohe	pram
hunúŋp nagmíyaŋpi	bike
ȟemáni	train
igmú	cat
iwátȟokšu	truck
iyéčhiŋkiŋyaŋke,	car
iyéčhiŋkyaŋke	car
iyók'iŋpa	traditional cradle
kiŋyékhiyapi	airplane
luhá	you have
matȟó	bear
matȟóla	bear cub
owáyawa itȟókšu	school bus
oyáte itȟókšu	bus
šúŋka	dog
šúŋkawakȟáŋ	horse
šuŋȟpála	puppy
thiíkčeya	tipi
thípi	house
tȟápa	ball
tȟaté kaȟwógyapi	kite
wáta	boat, ship
wóškate	toys, games
yuhá	he/she has

7. Hayápi   Clothes

čhegnáke	breech-cloth, loin cloth
čhuwígnaka, čhuwígnake	dress
háŋpa	shoes
haŋpíkčeka	moccasins
hayápi	clothes
huŋská	leggings
huŋyákȟuŋ	socks
iphíyake	belt
mahél úŋpi	underwear
múŋ	I wear
napíŋkpa	gloves
nitéhepi	skirt
núŋ	you wear
ógle háŋska	coat
ógle šóka	jacket
ógle zibzípela	T-shirt
ógle zigzíča	sweater
ógle	shirt
šiná	blanket
šináhiŋšma	buffalo robe
tȟahá čhuwígnaka	leather dress
tȟahá ógle	leather shirt
tȟahú iyápehe	neck scarf

úŋ	to wear
uŋzóǧe ptéčela	shorts
uŋzóǧe	pants
wanáp'iŋ	necklace
wapȟóštaŋ	hat
wapȟóštaŋla	cap

8. Thiwáhe Mitȟáwa kiŋ   My Family

Kinship terms of address:

até	father
čhiŋkší	son
čhiyé	boy's elder brother
čhuŋkší	daughter
čhuwé	girl's elder sister
iná	mother
kaká / lalá	grandfather (informal; southern / northern)
misúŋkala, misúŋ(ka)	younger brother (both girl and boys)
mitȟáŋkala (or tȟaŋká)	girl's younger sister
thibló	girl's elder brother
tȟakóža	grandchild
tȟaŋké	boy's elder sister
tȟaŋkší	boy's younger sister
tȟuŋkášila	grandfather (formal)
uŋčí	grandmother

9. Mitȟáŋčhaŋ   My Body

čhaŋkpé	knee
čhaŋté	heart
čhekpá	belly button
čhuwí	back
hiŋyéte	shoulder
hú	leg
istó	arm
išpá	elbow
makhú	chest
mayúkȟaŋ, mayúkȟe	I have (a body part)
napé	hand
napsúkaza	fingers
natá	head
niyúkȟaŋ, niyúkȟe	you have (a body part)
sí	foot
sičháŋ	thigh
siókaza	toes
thezí	stomach, belly
tȟahú	neck
tȟaŋčháŋ	body
uŋzé	buttock
yukȟáŋ	to have (a body part)

10. Waskúyeča na Watȟótȟo	Fruits and Vegetables
ƃló	potato
čhaŋpȟá	chokecherry
čhuŋwíyapehe	grape, grapevine
kȟáŋta	plums
kuŋkúŋ	cucumber
pȟaŋǧí zizí	carrot
psíŋ	onion
Táku waštéyalaka he?	What do you like?
híŋpsiŋla	turnip
ȟaspáŋ pȟéstola	pear
ȟaspáŋ zí	orange
ȟaspáŋ	apple
ŋžíŋžiŋtka	tomato
wagmúšpaŋšni	water melon
waȟpé iŋkpážiži	lettuce
waskúyeča	fruit
waštélakA	he / she likes
waštéwalakA	I like
waštéwalake šni	I don't like
watȟótȟo	vegetable, green growing things
wažúšteča, wazíškeča	strawberry
ičhágnaška	black currant
škopela	banana

1. Lakȟóta Makȟóčhe	Lakota Country
aŋpétu wí, áŋpa wí	sun
blé	lake
čhaŋkú	road, path
čhúŋšoke	forest
haŋhépi wí, haŋwí	moon
haŋté	cedar, juniper
ȟé	mountains
íyaŋ	stone
makȟá	earth, clay, ground
maȟpíya	cloud
maȟpíya	sky
obláye	plain
otȟúŋwahe	town
pahá	hill
pȟeží	grass
Táku waŋláka he?	What do you see?
pȟešládaka	cactus
waǧáčhaŋ	cottonwood
wakpá	river
wakpála	creek
waŋblákA	I see
waȟčá, wanáȟča	flower
waȟpé	leaf
wazí	pine
wičháȟpi	star
wičhóthi	village

12. Wóyute na Wóyatke	Food and Drink
aǧúyapi skuyéla	sweet roll
aǧúyapi	bread
asáŋpi sutá	cheese
asáŋpi	milk
bló ičhéǧuǧuyapi	French fries
čhaŋháŋpi	sugar
hoǧáŋ	fish
ímapuza	I am thirsty
Ínipuza he?	Are you thirsty?
ínipuza	you are thirsty
ípuza	he/she is thirsty
kapȟópapi	pop, coca cola
ločhíŋ	he/she is hungry
lowáčhiŋ	I am hungry
Loyáčhiŋ he?	Are you hungry?
loyáčhiŋ	you are hungry
mní	water
mniskúya	salt
omníča	beans
pápa	dried meat
psíŋ	rice
tȟaló yukpáŋpi	hamburger
tȟaló	meat
tȟaspáŋ haŋpí	apple juice
tȟaspáŋzi haŋpí	orange juice
wagmíza	corn
waháŋpi	soup
wakȟályapi	coffee
waȟpékȟalyapi	tea
wígli-uŋ-káǧapi	fry bread
wítka	eggs
wóyatke	drink
wóyute	food
wóžapi	pudding

13. Obláye Ektá	On the Plains
čhaŋšká	hawk (esp. red tailed)
gnugnúška	grasshopper
hečá	turkey vulture
ikpísaŋla	pronghorn
kimímela, kimímila	butterfly
maká	skunk
maštíŋska (maštíŋčala)	rabbit, jack rabbit (bunny)
pispíza	prairie dog
píško	night hawk
pȟahíŋ	porcupine
siŋtéȟla	rattlesnake
šuŋgmánitu	coyote
tȟáȟča	deer (mule deer)
tȟašíyagnuŋpa	meadowlark
tȟatȟáŋka	buffalo, buffalo bull
uŋkčépagmigma	dung beetle

wábloša	red-winged blackbird
wablúška	insect
wamákȟašaŋ	animal
waŋblí	eagle
zuzéča	snake

14. Takúku Íčhitȟokeča   Opposites

Use the illustrations and flashcards to teach the pairs of adjectives. Then you can use your surroundings to practice the new vocabulary, e.g. **Táku tȟáŋka makípazo wo/we!** {Show me something big}, **Táku spáya hwo/he?** {What is wet?} – **Wakpá; Mní** etc. Reinforce the vocabulary in classes at random, by saying one adjective of the pair and have the students respond to each other.

čhaŋtéšicA	sad
čhaŋtéwašte	glad
čhatkáyatakiya	to the left
čhépA	fat
číkʼala	small
čónala	few, little
eháke	last
háŋskA	long
henála, waníčA	empty
hótȟaŋkA	loud
ȟʼaŋhí	slow
iníla	quiet
išláyatakiya	to the right
káŋ	old (person, animal)
kapʼóžela	light, not heavy
khúta	down
khúžA	sick (Southern Lakota)
kȟátA	hot
lečhála	new (thing) (Southern Lakota)
natȟáka	close
lúzahaŋ (oȟʼáŋkȟo)	quick
óta	many, much
owáŋyaŋg šícA	ugly
owáŋyaŋg wašté	good looking
ožúla	full
pȟáŋžela	soft
ptéčela	short
púza	dry
šápA	dirty
šápe šni	not dirty, clean
šícA	bad
sní	cold
spáyA	wet
sutá	hard
tȟamáheča	skinny
tȟáŋkA	big
tȟaŋní, tȟaŋníla	old (thing)

tȟéča	young; new
tȟokáhe	first
tké	heavy
waŋkáta	up
wašté	good
wayázaŋ	sick (Northern Lakota)
yuǧáŋ	open
zaŋní	healthy

15. Wóžuthi Ektá   On the Farm

igmú	cat
iktómi	spider
itȟúŋkala	mouse
khukhúše	pig
kȟokhéyaȟʼaŋla	hen, chicken
Lená khukhúše héčapi.	These are pigs.
maǧá	goose
maǧáksica	duck
Ptegléška kiŋ sapsápapi.	The cows are black.
ptegléška, ptebléška	cow, cattle
šúŋka	dog
šúŋkawakȟáŋ	horse
Waglékšuŋ kiŋ núŋpapi.	There are two turkeys.
waglékšuŋ	turkey
wakíŋyela	pigeon, mourning dove

16. Miíte   My Face

hí	tooth, teeth
í	mouth
ihá	lip (especially lower lip)
ikhú	chin
ištá	eye, eyes
ištáȟehiŋ	eyebrow
ité	face
mayúkȟaŋ, mayúkȟe	I have (a body part)
nawáte	temple, temples
niyúkȟaŋ, niyúkȟe	you have (a body part)
núŋǧe	ears
osúŋ	braid, braids
pȟaȟté	forehead
pȟasú	nose
pȟehíŋ	hair
tȟahú	neck
tȟapȟúŋ	cheek
yukȟáŋ	to have (a body part)

17. Táku tókȟanuŋ he?   What are you doing?

This unit is based on verbs. In the K-2 level, teach should choose only a few of the most frequent verbs (up 6 at a time) and teach these with flashcard activities. H the children play games like this: 1) A child mimes a v the other children try to guess what it is and say the ver Lakota. 2) Mime the verb, but only when *Simon says*. A see the following unit, which reviews ten of the verbs.

With older or more advanced students, you can also introduce the 1ˢᵗ person singular forms (in parentheses).

…anáǧoptaŋ (anáwaǧoptaŋ)	to listen
…čhéyA (wačhéye)	to cry, to weep
…gnakA (éwagnake)	to put down on
…glastó (waglásto)	to comb one's hair
…glušlókA (waglúšloke)	to take off (clothes)
…akíč'uŋ (hawéč'uŋ)	to wear (clothes)
…hi-kpážaža (hi-wákpažaža)	to brush one's teeth
…čú (iwáču)	to take
…glúžaža (miglúžaža)	to wash
…háŋble (iwáhaŋble)	to dream
…ȟá (iwáȟa)	to smile
…gyaŋkA (waímnaŋke)	to run
…pútȟakA (iwáputȟake)	to kiss
…štíŋmA (ištíŋme)	to sleep
…tówapi owá (itówapi owáwa)	to draw a picture
…votakA (íblotake)	to sit down
…vúŋkA (imúŋke)	to go to bed
…aȟ'ól iyéyA (kaȟ'ól iyéwaye)	to throw
…igná (wégna)	to pet, to caress
…iktá (wékta)	to wake up, to get up
…ipázo (wépazo)	to show to
…'íŋ (wak'íŋ)	to carry
…'ú (wak'ú)	to give to
…áni (mawáni)	to walk
…ážiŋ (nawážiŋ)	to stand
…uŋwÁŋ (wanúŋwe)	to swim
…íži (owážiži)	to whisper
…áŋ (wapáŋ)	to yell
…ȟóskil yúzA (pȟóskil blúze)	to hug
…átA (waškáte)	to play
…ŋkákaŋyaŋkA (šuŋkákaŋmaŋke)	to ride a horse
…aŋyáŋkA (waŋbláke)	to see
…ayátkAŋ (wablátke)	to drink
…ayáwa (wabláwa)	to read
…óglakA (wówaglake)	to talk
…ótA (wáte)	to eat
…wa (wówawa)	to write, to draw
…ŋkÁ (maŋké)	to sit
…kȟápA (blukȟápe)	to catch
…ŋkÁ (muŋké)	to lie

…íčhita	policeman (Rosebud form)
…aŋksáyuha	policeman (Pine Ridge form)
…kšíla	boy
…la yaŋká yo/ye!	Be quiet!
…táku hwo/he?	Who/What are you?
…šíču wakȟáŋ	medical doctor
…šíču	white man
…úŋspekhiya	teacher

wawóyuspa	policeman (Cheyenne River form)
wičháȟčala	old man
wičháša	man
wičhíŋčala	girl
winúȟčala	old woman
wíŋyaŋ	woman

19. Thiyáta — At Home

čháŋ	wood; tree
čhowíŋža	floor
čhowíŋžakaȟpe	carpet
ikȟáŋčhola iwánaȟ'uŋ	radio
itówapi	picture, painting
mázaškaŋškaŋ	clock
mazóčhethi	stove
oákaŋke	chair, armchair
oákaŋke háŋska	sofa
omás'apȟe	telephone
ožáŋžaŋglepi	window
pšitȟó	beads
pȟetížaŋžaŋ, pȟetížaŋ	lamp
thitȟáhepiya	fan
thiyópa	door
thiyópa iyúhomni	door knob
wáglotapi	table
wápaha	staff
wíčalu	fan
wičhítenaškaŋškaŋ	television
wičhítowapi	pictures, photos

20. Wačhípi Ektá — At a Pow-Wow

čháŋčheǧa	drum
Eháŋk'ehaŋ Wačhí	Traditional Dance
Ékpazo Thimá Hiyúpi	Grand Entry
éyapaha	announcer
hóčhoka	inside dance arena
ikčé wačhí wičháša	male traditional dancer
ikčé wačhí wíŋyaŋ	female traditional dancer
ičábu	drum stick
íčalu	feather fan
lowáŋ wičháša	male singer
okȟá, okȟá wičháša	male singer, drum group
Oštéšteya Wačhí	Fancy Dance
owáčhi	dance arena
pȟéša	head roach
Snasná Wačhí	Jingle Dress Dance
Šiná Úŋ Wačhí	Shawl Dance
tȟahá čhuwígnaka úŋ	female traditional dancer
uŋkčéla káǧapi	feather bustle
Uŋzóǧela Wačhí	Grass Dance
wačhípi	pow-wow, dance, dancing
waháčhaŋka	shield

waȟpé wókheya	arbor
wápaha	flag
wawáŋyaŋke	spectators
wičháglata	female singer

21. Otȟúŋwahe Ektá   In Town

čhaŋksáyuha	policeman
ȟemáni	train
iwátȟokšu	truck
iyéčhiŋkiŋyaŋke	car
iyéčhiŋkyaŋke	car
iyéčhiŋkiŋyaŋke oáphiye	car repair
kiŋyékhiyapi	airplane
mas'óphiye	store, trading post
mázaska thípi	bank
očháŋku	road, street
oíčhimani thípi	hotel
okhúže thípi	hospital
owáčhekiye	church
owáyawa itȟókšu	school bus
owáyawa	school
owóte thípi	restaurant
oyáte itȟókšu	bus
oyúžužu thípi	post office
pȟéta oínažiŋ	fire station
thípi	house
wičhítenaškaŋškaŋ othí	cinema
wígli oínažiŋ	gas station
wówapi othí	library
wóyute mas'óphiye	grocery store

22. Tȟatúye Tópa   Four Directions

blokétu	summer
čháŋ	tree
Čhaŋnápȟopa Wí	February
Čhaŋpȟá Sápa Wí	July
Čhaŋwápe Ǧí Wí	September
Čhaŋwápe Kasná Wí	October
Čhaŋwápe Tȟó Wí	May
čhaŋwápe	tree leaf
Ištáwičhayazaŋ Wí	March
maǧážu	rain, it is raining
mačhúwita	I am cold
maȟpíya sápa	dark clouds/sky
okȟátA	it is hot
omákȟate	I am hot
omášte	the sun is shining
ošíčeča, ošíčečakA	bad weather
osní	it is cold
owáštečakA	good weather
Pȟeží Tȟó Wí	April
ptaŋyétu	fall
p'ó	fog

Thíŋpsiŋla Itkáȟča Wí	June
Tȟahé Kapšúŋ Wí	December
tȟaté	wind
tȟatúye	direction, wind flow
wá	snow
wáhiŋháŋ, wáhiŋhé	to snow
wakíŋyaŋ hotȟúŋpi	thunder
wakíŋyaŋ tuŋwáŋpi	lightning
Waníyetu Wí	November
waníyetu	winter
wasú hiŋháŋ	hail storm
Wasútȟuŋ Wí	August
wétu	spring
wígmuŋke	rainbow
Wiótheȟika Wí	January

23. Ȟeyáta   In the Mountains

Use the same activities as Unit 14.

halháta, uŋkčékhiȟa	magpie
heȟáka	elk, wapiti (male elk)
hiŋháŋ	owl
ȟoká	badger
igmútȟaŋka	mountain lion
itȟúŋkasaŋ	weasel
kȟaŋǧí	crow
matȟó	bear
šuŋǧíla	fox, red fox
tȟašnáheča	ground squirrel
tȟažúška	ant
upížata	swallow
wičhíteglega	raccoon
zičá	squirrels

Note: A few speakers gave iȟóka as a variant for badger.

24. Blé Ektá   At a Lake

Use the same activities as for Unit 14.

blóza	pelican
čhápa	beaver
čhapȟúŋka	mosquito
gnašká	frog
hoǧáŋ	fish
hoyázela	kingfisher
hoȟyázela, khušléča	kingfisher (variants)
matúška	crawfish
pȟatkáša	water turtle (western painte
khéya	snapping turtle
siŋkpȟé	muskrat
thuswéčha	dragonfly

Note: The "A" indicates that the final vowel in word may change from an "a" into an "e" or " under certain circumstances.

Classroom Instructions

Here is a list of instructions that teachers should use consistently.

Starting the Lesson

Ho, mitȟákožapi! – Hello, my grandchildren!

Ho, waŋná! – All right, now! (Let's start.)

Iyotaka yo/ye (po/pe)! – Sit down!

During the Lesson

Nážiŋ yo/ye (po/pe)! – Stand up!

Iyotaka yo/ye (po/pe)! – Sit down!

U wo/we (po/pe)! – Come here!

Wówapi kiŋ ičú wo/we (po/pe)!

    – Take out your books.

Wówapi kiŋ yuǧáŋ yo/ye (po/pe)! – Open the book!

Wówapi kiŋ él étuŋwaŋ yo/ye (po/pe)!

    – Look at the picture!

Wówapi waŋží owá yo/ye (po/pe)! – Draw a picture!

Anáǧoptaŋ yo/ye (po/pe)! – Listen!

Amakípazo wo/we (po/pe)! – Show me!

Wówapi kiŋ makípazo wo/we (po/pe)!

    – Show me the picture!

Lé ičú wo/we (po/pe)! – Take this!

Lečhiya waŋyáŋka yo/ye (po/pe)! – Look here!

Lakȟótiya wóglaka yo/ye (po/pe)! – Talk in Lakota!

Ihákab eyá yo/ye (po/pe)! – Say it after me!

Olé yo/ye (po/pe)! – Look it up! Find it!

Tókhe Lakȟótiya eyápi he?

    – How do they say it in Lakota?

Akhé! – Again! (Repeat!)

Yawá yo/ye (po/pe)! – Read it! / Count it!

Owá yo/ye! – Write it! / Draw it!

Aphé yo/ye (po/pe)! – Wait!

Inína yaŋká yo/ye (po/pe)! – Quiet please!

Ečhúŋ(pi) šni yo/ye! – Don't do that!

Encouragement and Positive Feedback

Taŋyáŋ ečhánuŋ(pi)! – You did it well!

Taŋyáŋ ehé! – You said it well!

Wašté ló/kštó. – It is good.

Líla wašté (yeló/kšto)! – Very well/good.

Encouragement to Improve

Wašté, akhé eyá yo/ye (po/pe)! – Good, say it again!

Akhé ečhúŋ wo/we (po/pe)! – Do it again!

Finishing an Activity

Niglúštaŋ he? – Are you finished?

Hó waŋná. – Time is up!

Waŋná iyéhaŋtu... – It is time for…

Philámayayapi! / Philámayaye. – Thank you.

Ending the Lesson

Ho, waŋná uŋkígluštaŋpi!

    – That's all! (We have finished!)

Waŋná henákča. – That's all for now!

Waŋná glá yo/ye (po/pe)!

    – Go home now! (if at the end of school day.)

Tókša híŋhaŋni kiŋ akhé. – See you again tomorrow.

Taŋyáŋ yá yo/ye (po/pe)! – Good bye!

Aŋpétu wašté yuhá yo/ye (po/pe)! – Have a nice
    day!

Taŋyáŋ glá yo/ye (po/pe)!

    – Go home well ("Good bye!").

A, a	aǧúyapi	{bread}		**N, n**	napé	{hand}
Aŋ, aŋ	aŋpáwi	{sun}		**O, o**	oákaŋke	{chair}
B, b	bébela	{baby}		**P, p**	pispíza	{prairie dog}
Č, č	čónala	{few}		**Ph, ph**	pheží	{grass}
Čh, čh	čhápa	{beaver}		**Pȟ, pȟ**	pȟahíŋ	{porcupine}
Č', č'	č'ó	{splashing sound}		**P', p'**	p'ó	{fog}
E, e	épazo	{to point at}		**S, s**	sí	{foot}
G, g	gnaška	{frog}		**Š, š**	šúŋka	{dog}
Ǧ, ǧ	ǧí	{brown}		**T, t**	tópa	{four}
H, h	hokšíla	{boy}		**Th, th**	thípi	{house}
Ȟ, ȟ	ȟé	{mountain}		**Tȟ, tȟ**	tȟuŋkášila	{grandfather}
I, i	igmú	{cat}		**T', t'**	t'á	{to die}
Iŋ, iŋ	íŋyaŋ	{rock}		**U, u**	úta	{acorn}
K, k	kimímela	{butterfly}		**Uŋ, uŋ**	uŋčí	{grandmother}
Kh, kh	khéya	{turtle}		**W, w**	wičhíŋčala	{girl}
Kȟ, kȟ	kȟáŋta	{plum}		**Y, y**	yámni	{three}
K', k'	k'á	{to dig}		**Z, z**	zičá	{squirrel}
L, l	lowáŋ	{to sing}		**Ž, ž**	žó	{to whistle}
M, m	matȟó	{bear}		**'**		(glottal stop)